Notes From a Buddhist Mystic

Daniel Scharpenburg

Golden Eternity Publications

ISBN: **0692277420**
ISBN-13:**978-0692277423**

DEDICATION

May All Beings Be Happy
May All Beings Be Free From Suffering

some of this content was originally published on
Elephantjournal.com

many thanks to all of the writers and editors there.

•

DANIEL SCHARPENBURG

CONTENTS

Introduction: vii
The Mystic (poem) xi
Why Buddhist Mystic: 15
A Note on Ch'an and Zen: 17
Some Basic Concepts: 19
Meditation Instructions: 29
Far Out Zen: 31
The Buddha: 35
Getting Out of Our Own Way: 41
Lost and Found: My Journey into Buddhism: 45
The Buddha as a Revolutionary Figure: 55
I am Enlightened and So Are You: 65
On Taking Refuge: 71
The Revolutionary Nature of the 4 Noble Truths: 75
Is All of Life Suffering?: 87
Excavation: 93
Biohacking: 97
4:30 AM: 101
Commit to Sit: 103
Unleash Your Buddha Nature: 109
The Four Immeasurables: 113
The Intellect is Part of the Problem: 117
Six Perfections: 121
Bedtime Meditation Club: 129
Buddha and Religion: 135

Ikkyu: Zen Rebel: 139
Meaning of Ch'an: 145
Three Essentials: 155
The Legend of Bodhidharma: 157
Two Entries: 163
Huineng, Illiterate Monk: 167
Pang, Enlightened Dad: 173
Dogen: 179
Suzuki Shosan, Fierce Zen: 187
Xu Yun, Preserver of Ch'an: 193
We All Want to Change the World: 199
Bones of the Buddha Statue: 201
Buddha in the Land of the Pagans: 205

INTRODUCTION

When I was a kid I wanted to be a writer. True story. Not because I had some creative urge, but because I thought writers had it easy. I thought writers just sat around writing all day and didn't have to really work. That was my idea when I was very young. Anyone who writes knows that is ridiculous. But youth comes with many ridiculous ideas. I had a childhood friend who really wanted to be an actor for the same reason. I'm sure he was also wrong, although he did run off to Hollywood when he grew up and he acts in a few commercials and minor things.

At any rate, at some point in my life I just stopped writing. Maybe it was all the writing I had to do to get an English degree. Who knows. But within the fast few years I started writing again. I tried to write a novel and that didn't go so well. I tried to write some poetry and that didn't go so well either. I tried to write about my political views and that was a failure too.

But then there was something else I found the will

to write about: religion.

Well, I don't really call it religion. How about the Dharma? Or the Dharma of the Buddha? Because it's not the same as religion, but also it is. OOOH. That's hard to wrap our minds around.

I started meditating over ten years ago and after a few years I officially became a Buddhist. Buddhism spoke to me on a deep and personal level and I felt pulled to it in a way that I couldn't have resisted even if I had tried. One of my teachers said that he suspected that it was related to Karma from a previous life. I'm not sure about all that, but I do know that becoming a Buddhist and taking different Buddhist vows was something I couldn't resist.

So I started a blog and I wrote about Buddhist concepts for a little while, especially my personal journey. I submitted some articles to an online magazine called Elephant Journal.

I became a regular contributor. It turns out I can endlessly write about this subject. Article after article after article came out of me and they continue to come.

They say the Dharma cannot be expressed in words.

Yet we keep trying to do just that.

One of my heroes, Zen Master Dogen, wrote a work called the Shobogenzo, or Treasury of the True Dharma Eye. He spent thousands and thousands of pages elucidating concepts that can't be explained in words. I'm nowhere near the writer he was, but I can only hope to be half as prolific.

I've included personal stories, lists of Buddhist virtues, and stories of great Zen masters. These are all just floating around at different points in the text, the Zen masters appear in chronological order except for Ikkyu, my favorite. He appears ahead of the others.

I hope you enjoy this collection. Some of it is from my work at Elephant Journal, some of it is from my blog, and some of it is original content that hasn't been published anywhere.

It's a bit of a mixture of different kinds of things, but I've tried to place the general meditation and Buddhism things at the beginning and the Ch'an/Zen specific things towards the end.

One more note: I use the term 'Mahayana' several times. It's a term for a large sect of Buddhism that includes many smaller branches including Ch'an,

Pure Land, Tendai, and many others.

To put it as simply as possible: Mahayana Buddhism is centered in the belief that our true nature is Enlightened already.

I'll go into that concept a great deal in this book.

Enjoy.

THE MYSTIC

With one foot in the realm of emptiness and one in the realm of form, the Mystic dwells.

The Mystic is a spiritual excavator, digging in, penetrating reality, cutting away the things that aren't really present to find the Truth.

The Mystic walks a path, not of belief or devotion, but of transformation, spiritual revolution, awakening, unleashing true potential.

The Mystic dwells in a state of Dreamy Wonder, seeing the world as wonderful and wonder-filled.

The Mystic tends to see words like 'religious', 'spiritual', and even 'God' as ultimately insufficient to explain the beautiful wondrous nature of the Universe. Words fail to describe Ultimate Reality.

The Mystic is a seer, always seeing the world through different eyes, with a broad view of the world instead of a narrow one.

The Mystic dwells in luminous emptiness, understanding that wisdom tells me I am nothing and love tells me I am everything.

The Mystic is a spiritual seeker, always on the journey to accumulate more wisdom, never finished learning and practicing.

The Mystic seeks Unity and is devoted to dissolving barriers, bringing beings together instead of tearing them apart.

The Mystic sees the Divine and Sacred in all things.

The Mystic sees the world as connected and bound together by love. If love is all then love is everyone.

The Mystic sees the Seed of Enlightenment in all beings and blesses them all as Buddhas-to-be.

The Mystic travels to Ultimate Reality, bringing a little back every time.

I am the Mystic.

You can be too.

If you're open to it.

DANIEL SCHARPENBURG

WHY BUDDHIST MYSTIC?

People don't know what the word mystic means anymore, most of the time. When I told one person that I was a mystic he asked if I was a wizard. Here is the definition I use.

Mystic: a person who seeks unity or oneness with the absolute through contemplative practices and/or self surrender, or who believes in spiritual truths that are beyond the intellect and beyond labels.

There have been mystics in all cultures and throughout history. There have been Christian mystics like Emmanuel Swedenborg and Meister Eckhart. There have been Muslim mystics like Rumi. Some have argued that Jesus was a Jewish mystic.

I find a great difference between a Mystic and a Religious Person.

The Buddha was a mystic. He was trying to penetrate ultimate reality. Ultimate reality in a

Buddhist context is sometimes defined as oneness and sometimes defined as emptiness. That's because it is difficult to grasp. We should expect it to be difficult to grasp because it's ultimate reality.

And I don't want to be like Buddha so much as I want to do what he did. I want to engage with Ultimate Reality. We usually call it Enlightenment. And it's available to us right now.

So, why do I call myself a Mystic?

Mainly because I'm not a monk. Some Buddhists have monastic vows that they take and I don't. I am, nevertheless, really devoted to Buddhist practice. I've taken Bodhisattva Vows, which involves taking it upon myself to save all beings.

Buddhism is not theistic or atheistic. It's pantheistic. All things are sacred. It's not a path of salvation. It's a path of TRANSFORMATION.

I'm constantly engaged in furthering my mystical life.

I don't seek to follow in the footsteps of the Buddha or anyone else. Not really. I seek what they sought.

A NOTE ON CH'AN AND ZEN

I am a member of a Buddhist lineage that is called Ch'an. It is a Chinese branch of Mahayana Buddhism that claims to go back to a specific teaching from the Buddha.

In the West we call it Zen. Zen was the Japanese version and we call it Zen because Japanese Buddhists were the first ones to bring it to both the United States and Europe.

The proper name is Ch'an. Although it's thought that Ch'an might itself be a mistranslation of a sanskrit word, dhyana. Which means meditation.

Except for very few people, no one has ever heard the word Ch'an in the United States and Europe. Some even call it 'Chinese Zen'.

You'll notice throughout this book that I alternate. Sometimes I call it Ch'an and sometimes I call it Zen.

I've tried to call it Zen when referring to Japanese Buddhists and Ch'an when referring to Chinese

Buddhists. But, I'm sure I've made a few mistakes along the way and for that I apologize. I hope you don't get confused.

SOME BASIC CONCEPTS

So, if you know a lot about Buddhism already, you can skip this. I'm writing this chapter to catch anyone up to speed who knows very little about Buddhism. Some of these ideas will end up repeating later.

Here we go:

What Buddhism is NOT:

Buddhism does not support the concept of belief in deities. In this sense, it is sometimes called an atheistic religion. Atheism is kind of a loaded term, created by theists to describe "those who don't believe what we believe". Pagan is another term like this, created by Christians to define those whose beliefs do not descend from Abraham. I prefer not to use loaded terms such as these. I'd rather call it Pantheistic, ie everything is sacred. Buddhism teaches that all things are interdependent. An external god figure would go against this belief because then all things would be dependent upon said god figure.

Also, Buddhism is not all that concerned with life after death. One of Buddha's disciples asked him what happened when we die and he said, "I am more concerned with what happens here."

Now, I know someone is about to say, "don't buddhists believe in reincarnation?" The answer is, most don't. Tibetan Buddhists do and there is a group from China called Pure Land Buddhists that do, but overall, most Buddhists do not really believe in reincarnation. Or, rather, if reincarnation exists it's not nearly as simple as we usually think of.

Buddha used the Hindu concept of Karma often as a metaphor in his teachings. Karma in a Buddhist context simply means that what you do, good or bad, affects everyone, including yourself. IE, if you do something bad, it makes the world a slightly worse place for everyone, including yourself. So, it's in all of our best interests to be kind to one another. That's it. Not some magical force that causes you to suffer for misdeeds or anything of that nature. Your karma is said to live on after your death because what you do affects the world for a very long time after you are gone.

Buddha railed against the Hindu belief in transmigration of souls. He didn't really believe in souls. He taught that our identity is really only a combination of five things. They are: the body, feelings, mental formations, perception, and consciousness. Because it seems unlikely that all of these things survive death together in order to pass on, he considered life after death unlikely. This philosophy came from simply thinking deeply about the answer to the question: "Who am I?"

What Buddhism is:

I describe it as a mystical path devoted to the cultivation of Morality, Wisdom, and Concentration. Every Buddhist teaching can fit into at least one of those categories, and usually more than one.

Buddha taught that all things are basically inherently unified. IE nothing exists on it's own. All things are interdependent. In a sense, we are all one. Nothing exists apart from anything else. Everything is dependent upon or caused by something else, and this ultimately connects all things. The Buddhist concept of compassion is supported by this idea. If we are all one, then your suffering is my suffering as well. So, to harm you would essentially be the same as harming myself. Realizing that all things are one is a peaceful and wondrous experience. All feelings of loneliness are replaced by a feeling of being a part of something....a part of everything..

The core teaching of Buddhism is the four noble

truths:

The Four Noble Truths

All life is suffering

The cause of suffering is attachment

The cessation of suffering is possible

It is possible through self transformation by the Eightfold Path

1. All life is suffering, or life ain't easy.

Life is a constant struggle for everyone. No matter who you are, you suffer losses far too often. Everyone hurts, everyone gets sick, everyone loses loved ones, everyone dies. This cannot be stopped. Life hurts.

The origin of suffering is attachment, or, Why do I always want what I can't have?

Life is this way for several reasons. Part of the problem is that we are always thinking about what we want. We are craving the things we don't have. We get stuck in the trap of: "if I can just achieve these goals, then I will be happy". This is a problem because when we are stuck in this trap, then we are unable to be happy without achieving these goals. We are stressed and miserable because of what we don't have. And, this part is important, no matter how many of our goals are achieved, we will always want more. That's why rock stars and millionaires turn to drugs or kill themselves sometimes. They get to a point where they have everything they thought they ever wanted, and they still want more.

The cessation of suffering is attainable, or the sun will come out.

This can be stopped. All you have to do is learn to appreciate the things you have and learn how to relax. Nirvana means freedom from all worries, troubles, and complexes. The actual problems of life don't go away, but we can learn how to handle them better and still be happy.

The path to cessation is the Eightfold Path.

The path to the end of suffering is like a roadmap. If we follow it, the results will be predictable. It is called the middle path, between the extremes of excessive self indulgence and excessive self denial.

The Eightfold Path.

Right View

Seeing things as they really are. Realizing that everyone else suffers just like you. Realizing that all things are connected.

Right Intention

Commitment to ethical and mental self improvement

Right Speech

Not lying and not saying things to hurt the feelings of others.

Right Action

Do not harm others (ie, be a pacifist), do not steal, do not take life (some take this to mean that you should be a vegetarian, others do not), do not lie, abstain from sexual misconduct (ie, no cheating, no tricking women into sleeping with you, etc.)

Right Livelihood

Earn your living in a good way that is both legal and peaceful. Don't have a job that harms or exploits others.

Right Effort

To do everything for wholesome and good reasons.

Right Mindfulness

Pay attention to the processes that your mind goes through as much as possible. Often, we see things and make judgments, only halfway thinking about what we've seen.

Right Concentration
Unifying and focusing our mind upon each wholesome action that we undertake. We are often distracted by other things and only halfway think about what we're doing. Buddhism teaches us that we can exercise and strengthen our mind's ability to do this through meditation.

To sum it up simply, we could say that the cause of most of our suffering is our own ego and selfishness. We spend far too much time wishing to get the things we want and worrying about losing them and this causes us to suffer. In reality, nothing lasts forever and we're a lot better off if we accept that.

Now, you might say, 'that doesn't sound like a religion at all'. A lot of people think that. There is an endless amount of debate regarding whether Buddhism is a religion, a philosophy, or something else. As I said, I think of it as a mystical path.

Is Buddhism a religion?

I don't think so.

If by religion you mean a system of worship or blind faith, then no, Buddhism is not a religion. I don't worship anything. Buddhism isn't about worshiping, fearing, or loving some divine figure. Because Buddhism doesn't try to answer supernatural questions, I know several people that practice Buddhism alongside other religions.

We have meditation instead of prayer. Meditation leads to self control, purification, and enlightenment. It's all about looking within yourself.

Buddhism is also non-dogmatic. Skepticism is considered a great virtue. The Buddha consistently said that we should think for ourselves and test things instead of simply accepting them. He wanted all of his teachings to be held up to careful scrutiny.

Buddhism is not the source of a divine revelation. The founder of Buddhism was a normal man, just like you and I. All he taught was suffering and the way out of suffering. That is all we teach. The whole point is we can do what he did.

If religion has to involve a belief in a god or gods, or some other supernatural phenomena, then Buddhism is not one.

But, if religion is defined more broadly, then things are more complicated.

If religion means:

a shared set of beliefs and practices

or

Our search for spirituality

27

or

Our search for transcendence

or

Our search for our fundamental role in the world...

then Buddhism does indeed qualify.

My conclusion?

Labels like: religion, philosophy, or even spirituality probably aren't all that helpful. It's part of human nature to try to put things into nice and neat little categories. Reality rarely fits into such categories.

MEDITATION INSTRUCTIONS

Sit in a comfortable and quiet place. Sit in the full lotus or half lotus position. If both of those positions are too difficult, regular cross-legged sitting is fine. The full lotus is the feet placed on top of the knees. The half lotus is one foot placed on one knee.

Adjust your posture so that your spine is erect. Allow the rest of your body to be relaxed around your upright spine. Rest your hands in your lap or on your legs. Allow your eyes to gently close. Bring your full attention to the sensations of sitting still. Allow your breathing to be natural. Bringing attention to your head, release any tension in your face and relax your jaw. Relax your neck and shoulders. Feel the rise and fall of your abdomen with each breath. Bring attention all the way down through your body.

Bringing your attention to the present experience, acknowledge the full range of phenomena that are happening in this moment. Think of all the sensations that are present. Allowing all of your

29

experiences to be as they are, redirect your attention to the sensations of breathing. Let other sensations fall into the background. Take a few moments to investigate where you feel the breath coming and going most easily. Make the breath your point of focus.

Breathing in, know that you are breathing in. Breathing out, know that you are breathing out. Acknowledge your in and out breathing. Each time your attention wanders away to some stray thought, gently redirect it to your breath.

Continue to follow your breath.
This is meditation. I suggest starting with five minutes a day and incrementally increasing to thirty. Or more. Don't let me hold you back.

It seems simple, but inside our heads is a crazy person that wants to do anything but pay attention to the present moment.

FAR OUT ZEN

Ikkyu Sojun is my personal hero. I talk about how much I like him pretty often.

He was the embodiment of iconoclastic Zen. He rebelled against many of the monks and Zen teachers of his time who had become corrupted by politics are greed. He called out the practice of selling Enlightenment certificates. His Zen wasn't held down by needless structure and tradition. It was about just this moment, real ultimate reality. Mystical truth, not religion.

That's what he's known for. But he did something else as well. He took Zen teaching to places that had no experience of it. Most of his contemporaries gave teachings only to monks. Ikkyu wasn't like that. Not content to live in a monastery, he took Zen into the world. His temple was the street. And he taught people that monks would never teach. He taught Zen practice to prostitutes, artists, homeless

31

people, and alcoholics. He brought the Dharma to the misfits and radicals, those who were looked down on by society.

I'm no Ikkyu. I couldn't possibly live up to his legacy. He is a legendary figure. But, I want to do what he did. I want to take the Dharma to strange places. I am bringing the teachings to Poets and Artists, Pagans and Hippies, Radicals and Misfits. I am not content to sit in a Zen temple 'preaching to the choir', talking about Zen with people who are as boring as I am.

I want to bring Zen to people who burn like roman candles, to people who are not ordinary.

Ikkyu called his Zen 'Furyu', which means Far Out.

Here in the modern era the phrase 'Far Out' brings to mind images of hippies from the 1960s. It's easy to picture a long-haired man in a tie dye t-shirt holding up a peace sign and saying, "Far Out Zen, man."

And that's okay. With the ideals of peace, love, equality and rebellion that the hippie movement represents, I don't think Ikkyu would have a problem with the connection.

Zen is Far Out.

I'm going to call my Zen the same thing my hero Ikkyu called his.

Welcome to Far Out Zen.

DANIEL SCHARPENBURG

THE BUDDHA

Siddhartha Gautama, the man who would become the Buddha, went to sit under a tree. He had been a spiritual seeker for years and every path he had chosen had come to nothing. He was deeply unsatisfied with the mainstream religion of his time, which was anti-science and hostile to women and minorities.

So, he had traveled for years looking for spiritual truth.

And he hadn't found it. Many of us would have given up.

But, he sat under a tree. He had realized a small insight that had inspired him to look within himself for the truth. He had caught a glimpse of what we call our Buddha Nature.

So, he sat under this tree and meditated.

He didn't invent meditation. It had existed

for a very long time. People may not realize
that Buddhism is part of a continuum, it
builds on the religious teachings that
preceded it.

He was a die-hard meditation enthusiast. He
vowed to sit under that tree until he had a
breakthrough, some fundamental insight into
human suffering and the nature of reality.

and he sat

and he sat

and he sat

and he cleared his mind

and he cleared his mind

and he cleared his mind

And the truth came to him. At this point, he
became the Buddha, which means
'awakened one'.

He looked up at the sky and saw a star
twinkling and he said, "Look, I am

twinkling."

He realized fundamental truths on both a mundane level and on a deeper level.

He discovered that the source of our suffering is our craving, our endless state of wanting more and he described a path to overcome that suffering. This is the path that we still follow today. It teaches us that harming ourselves or others is counterproductive. It teaches us to think before we act, but also that thinking too much is often a problem. Who among us hasn't suffered due to excessive worrying.

He taught us to live in the present moment, rather than spending too much time in the past or future. This doesn't mean we should forget the past. There's a difference between learning from our mistakes and replaying them in our minds over and over forever. Of course we should learn from the past. We just shouldn't live there.

And the Buddha taught us that all things are interconnected. We tend to think that we are

37

separate from each other and from the world around us. This delusion is a great source of suffering in our lives. We are deeply connected to everything around us in countless ways. That's why negativity and destructiveness are harmful. When we put violence into the world, we are harming ourselves too. And when we put kindness and joy into the world, we are making things better for everyone. This includes ourselves.

And the Buddha thought to himself, "This insight I have is purely my own experience. I don't think I can teach this to anyone. They would have to see for themselves."

He considered staying, living out his life, alone in the wilderness. He was right, of course. Having an intellectual understanding of the Buddha's teaching isn't the same as enlightenment. We have to have a deeper understanding, an intuitive understanding rather than a philosophical one.

The Buddha was moved by a great sense of compassion. He thought teaching wouldn't work, but not trying seemed unacceptable.

So, he came out of the forest to teach us all
how to save ourselves from suffering.

It reminds me of a vow we sometimes take in
Mahayana Buddhism. It's attributed to a man named
Shantideva.

It's called the Bodhisattva Vow.

It's a vow that I have taken. It's usually translated
like this:

Beings are numberless; I vow to save them.
Delusions are inexhaustible; I vow to end
them.
Dharma gates are boundless; I vow to enter
them.
Buddha's Way is unsurpassable; I vow to
become it.

The Buddha came out of the wilderness to teach
even though it seemed impossible that anyone
would understand his teaching.

For those of us that take Bodhisattva Vows, it's similar. Saving all being is clearly something I cannot do, but I vow to do it anyway.

GETTING OUT OF OUR OWN WAY

Our true self is always open and free. The only thing stopping us from realizing that truth is ourselves.

We get in our own way. This applies not just to our spiritual practice, but to many of our goals in life, the big goals and the smaller goals. We are the cause of many of our own problems. Not all of our problems, but a lot more of them than we usually tend to realize.

The number one way of getting out of our own way is simply becoming aware. We meditate to train our awareness. We want to become more aware of ourselves and the things we do. If we simply can understand what we are doing, the ways we get in our own way, then solutions become easier for us to find.

How do we get in our own way? In Buddhism we talk about the Three Poisons–

greed, aversion and delusion. These three poisons all come from within us and they cause us a lot of our suffering. When we are guided by these poisons, we are causing ourselves to suffer. We are probably causing others to suffer as well.

The first poison is called greed. It's sometimes called desire or attachment as well. I want, I need, give it to me, please, please please I really want it. I need to get it and I need to figure out a way to get it. Maybe I can just take it.

Greed interrupts the natural flow of things. Adding my desire into the equation of life, trying to change or alter the way things are to bring me satisfaction, ultimately can lead to suffering. We often want things that we don't need and we sometimes want them so much that we get upset. We also sometimes want things that are incredibly unrealistic.

Aversion is the second poison. It's sometimes called Hatred. Aversion is essentially rejection. Get that thing away from me. Hatred and aversion arise in

42

response to something we don't like or want to happen to us. It often leads us to push away, at worst culminating in violence. Hatred and anger can overwhelm us, causing us to act in negative ways in order to get relief from these feelings. Sometimes pain can't be avoided, of course, but we make things worse for ourselves when we get angry or stressed out about it. Obviously bad things are going to happen and we want to avoid them and we should try, but at the same time, we shouldn't become obsessed about bad things. We tend to worry about things that are unrealistic too. And we tend to magnify things. If something bad happens and we get angry, we are making ourselves suffer more. Anger doesn't help. It only contributes to our negative feelings.

The third poison is ignorance. It's sometimes called delusion. This poison follows directly from the other two. Our greed and anger leads us to a sense of separation. To live with that separation I make up a story or narrative to explain who I am and why my greed and anger are justified. More and more of my true self is lost and I live in the dream of my narrative. This is a fundamental delusion. The more rigid we become trying to justify and bolster our story, the more we suffer, and the more we cause suffering for those around us.

So what can we do about this?

Awareness. Moment-to-moment awareness is what we talk about in Buddhism. If my mind is here and now, living in this moment instead of in some kind of delusional fantasy, then I am not polluted by the three poisons. Things are going to happen. The universe is going to unfold however it unfolds. We can't control everything. The only thing you can really and truly control is yourself. We can control how we respond to things. Sometimes it can be very difficult. Understanding your own actions and responses is the first step in getting out of your own way. It is a big step.

If we practice meditation, we can learn to be more aware of our minds. This is important.

LOST AND FOUND

"To study Buddhism is to study ourselves. To study ourselves is to forget ourselves"

-Dogen

I sometimes wonder if losing my parents has been a contributing factor in my interest in Buddhism, if their deaths led me to the path that I now found myself.

I was raised with Christianity, like most people are in the United States, but my upbringing wasn't particularly religious or spiritual. We went to church every Sunday for much of my childhood, but we didn't really talk about God at home.

45

I was fourteen years old when the cancer was discovered in my father's esophagus. The doctors put together a plan. They would do surgery and remove his stomach. I didn't know we could live without a stomach, but we can.

But when they cut him open, they discovered that the cancer was too widespread. So they just sewed him up again and started chemotherapy. This is actually not an incredibly rare thing to happen with stomach cancer, especially back then in the 1990s.

He lived for eleven months. I watched my mother take care of him and I saw him at what was almost certainly the lowest point in his life. First he lost his hair, then he lost a lot of weight. Before his death he looked like he had been in a famine or something. I saw a man die from cancer and I got to know all about suffering and impermanence firsthand.

Four years later, during my first year of college, it was like lightning struck our family again. My mother was diagnosed with lung cancer. Just like dad, they decided surgery wasn't an option and they put her on chemotherapy. Just like dad, I watched her body slowly fall apart until she died. The difference was this time I had to take care of her. It was hard. I had to drop out of college that year and put off my education for a little while. But, my mother needed me so I was there. I had to become an adult when I became parent-less. Some people don't become adults until a few years into their twenties, or even later. I didn't have that option.

The realities of suffering and impermanence are important concepts in Buddhism. I experienced those realities firsthand as a teenager. I watched each of my parents die slow and painful deaths. I think that's why I started thinking about deep questions regarding suffering and the causes of suffering. The religion I was raised with didn't seem to really be helpful in reducing my suffering. I imagine it does for some people, but it didn't seem to be that much help to me.

I didn't deal with their deaths very well and I ended up suffering from terrible anxiety and depression. I withdrew into myself. I started avoiding social situations. I just wanted to be alone and feel sorry for myself. I pushed away everyone that cared about me. I think I was afraid but I didn't really understand my feelings at the time. I lost my parents. If I let someone else be close to me, I could lose them. It's not a healthy attitude, but I think it is something a lot of people suffer from when they have to deal with a loss, especially when they

48

experience losses during teenage years.

I was drifting through college life. I took some random classes. I didn't choose a major. I didn't really have any direction in my life. I wasn't so much sad as just numb. My heart felt blank. I felt emptiness within. I still went through the motions of a normal college life, but I was just letting things happen to me. I was just carried along by life.

I took a World Religions class. It was there that things changed for me. I had no interest in religion before this class. I just took it because I thought it would be easy. Something in the story of the Buddha resonated deeply with me. I started reading all the books about Buddhism and meditation that I could. I started a daily meditation practice and it brought me out of my depression after a few weeks.

I started learning to accept loss.

The Buddha didn't experience anything like I did, of course. If anything, his experience was the opposite. He was shielded from all kinds of suffering by his protective father. His mother had died when he was a baby, but he had never known her, so even that loss didn't really affect him. He had every possible joy available to him for his entire life. That's not something most of us can relate to very well. He was royalty and his father was more protective than most. He made sure all of the greatest things were available and Siddhartha, the young Buddha-to-be never experienced loss.

The 13th century Japanese Zen master Dogen, on the other hand, had an entirely different experience from the Buddha. He was inspired by personal tragedy and I find his story to be something I can relate to and understand. He lost his father at the age of 2 and his mother at the age of 7. He became a young orphan and that is how he learned the realities of suffering and impermanence, just as I did as a teenager.

I lost my father when I was 15 and my mother when I was 19. Not nearly as young as Dogen, but certainly before I was ready to become a full adult. I think any child suffers a great deal when their parents pass before their time.

On her deathbed, Dogen's mother recognized the purity of her son's heart. She told him to devote his life to benefiting others. My mother told me the same thing on her deathbed. She said to me, "Always be a good person. Be kind to others."

Dogen's experience of great suffering inspired him to become a Buddhist monk. He devoted his life to understanding suffering, just as the Buddha had 1800 years earlier. He developed great compassion and an inquiring mind. I developed these as well. Was it the result of personal tragedy? I suppose there's no way to tell, but his story really speaks to me on a personal level.

Dogen went on to become a very important figure in Zen Buddhism, even founding his own sect. I don't truly want to compare myself to him. I only wanted to say that I find parallels between his story and my own.

Did the deaths of my parents cause me to search for spiritual truths and ultimately find Buddhism? I think so. So many people in the world never start asking deep questions like: why are we here? What causes suffering? What is reality?

It's just not something many people consider.

The suffering caused by loss led me to ask those questions.

BUDDHA AS A REVOLUTIONARY FIGURE

We tend to look at the Buddha as a serene
and calm figure. Generally we see statues
and pictures of him with a beatific look on
his face. Maybe his eyes are half open.
Maybe he's smiling.

That is good. Clearly we would all like to be
calm and serene in spite of life's troubles.
But I propose a different way of looking at
the Buddha. I look at the Buddha as a
counter-cultural icon. Like many other
historical figures, he saw the way things
were in his day and decided that we could
do better. He was a revolutionary who
proposed new ideas that changed the world
because he saw that the world needed to
change.

The Buddha was born in a time and place in
which society and culture were dominated
by a specific religious dogma. This
dominant religion was oppressive to
minorities and women and hostile toward

55

science. It is a good thing we don't have anything like that going on today. That would be hard to deal with.

The Buddha was a spiritual teacher and founder of a great religion, there is no doubt about that. But, he was also a revolutionary figure. He saw a religion and culture that were harmful and he stood up to them. He didn't have to do that. The easy answer would have been to gain spiritual insights and walk away from society. Many others had done so before him and at the time of his enlightenment, he did consider doing that. He decided to teach others and spread his insight to help the world, instead of keeping it to himself.

Siddhartha Gautama grew up in a very comfortable environment, far more comfortable than most of us can imagine. His father was a wealthy noble. Siddhartha was constantly surrounded by the best food, music, and beautiful women. He had a life of luxury that few people have.

He should have been happy, but he was not. Like many in the hippie movement of the 1960s, he wanted to leave his comfortable life behind to look for something more, something greater and more open. He was not unlike the many counter-cultural revolutionaries who were inspired by Jack Kerouac's 'On the Road', to leave behind their comfortable suburban lives in order to travel and see what else the world had to offer. Although his lifestyle was wonderful, he felt like a prisoner. He wasn't content with what society taught him that he was supposed to be. He didn't want to grow up to be a ruler like his father. He wanted to find his own way in life. As soon as he became aware of the great amount of suffering in the world, he became determined to leave his father's home and figure out something to do about it.

It should be noted that India in the Buddha's time was not a place with a lot of freedom. They had a rigid caste system that essentially defined your life from birth. The caste system was religiously inspired. The teachings of the Vedic religion, which would eventually evolve into Hinduism, defined the caste system. This religion was dominant to such an extent that Siddhartha didn't know how to go forward with his plan while living in the framework of normal society.

He was unhappy with the path his life seemed destined to take, and so he stepped off the path. He simply walked away from society, challenging the prevalent norm that it was his duty to carry on his father's legacy.

But he wasn't alone. There was a counterculture at the time. There were spiritual seekers who wanted to find religious truths in the world. They weren't content with the answers that the Vedic religion was providing, so they went off on their own. They felt that they had no choice but to drop out of society. Siddhartha was not the first to look around and say, "There must be more to life than this," but some of his ideas would galvanize the counterculture and change the world forever.

In Siddhartha's time, many people were beginning to become disillusioned by the Vedic religion. It's just that most of them were unwilling to challenge the boundaries.

But some were.

He tried to learn from different spiritual teachers for six years. He realized that no one had the answers he was looking for. The real spiritual revolution began when he realized that the truth was within him... within all of us. So, he didn't really need to learn the truth from someone else.

Even the best teachers can only show us the door. We have to walk through it ourselves.

So, with a new sense of determination, Siddhartha decided to look within himself for the truth. This was also a revolutionary idea. Even today, it still is. In most belief structures people tend to think that the ultimate reality, the truth, is somewhere outside of themselves. Many people tend to think that the truth is to be found by following some outside entity that they call God or by reading some scripture or listening to clergy.

Siddhartha decided that the truth was within.

So, using some meditation techniques that he had learned, he tried to look within himself for the answer. He sat underneath a big tree and resolved to sit there in quiet meditation until he had a great spiritual insight into the truth.

Siddhartha became enlightened. He took the title 'Buddha' which means the Enlightened One. He realized ultimate truths about the human condition. His first instinct was to simply live in seclusion for the rest of his life. He didn't think that the truths that he had discovered were things that people would want to hear. We live our lives mired in delusion and sometimes we are afraid of the truth. That's just part of how we live as human beings. He thought that he couldn't teach what he had learned to anyone.

Ultimately he decided that it was too important. Even though he wasn't sure that anyone would listen and understand, he had an obligation to try to spread his teachings, which we call the Dharma. It was his compassion that motivated him. He knew it was likely to be difficult, but there were so many suffering people in the world and he felt a sense of duty to try and help them.

The Buddha had discovered, in his calm state of insightful meditation, fundamental truths about our lives.

We are all interconnected. We tend to think of ourselves as individuals, separate from everything and everyone around us. That is simply not the case. We are all one. And deep down we all know this. He called our true nature our Buddha Nature and he said that we all have it within us. Our problem is that we have to get through our delusions to become aware of our true selves. And the most important thing is this: anyone can do it. Enlightenment isn't the province of an elite few. We can all become enlightened, in fact we are already.

Part of the significance of the Buddha's story is that he was just a man. He was a human being who attained Enlightenment and we can too.

He also said something even more shocking. He said that even women can become enlightened. Women have Buddha Nature just like men. That might be the most unique thing about Buddhism among the ancient religions. Any study of religions that have been around a long time tends to show that women are often not considered equal to men. We can say that this is because religions are a product of history and culture. That's true, but the Buddha was able to see beyond this when he said women could attain Enlightenment.

These ideas were revolutionary. As I mentioned, this was a rigidly stratified society. Hereditary priests called Brahmins were believed to have a monopoly on spiritual truth. Then, here comes this iconoclast saying that we can all become enlightened. A few old traditionalist men wanted things to stay the way they were, but this young charismatic spiritual teacher came and smashed all of that.

The Brahmins believed in worshiping fire and paying homage to the Gods. The Buddha questioned both of these ideas. He said, "I don't teach about Gods. I teach about suffering and the way out of suffering." He made the argument that our purpose isn't to worry about why we're here or what made us. Our purpose is to figure out the best way to live, that a mindful life is important. Reality is what matters. How you keep your mind from moment to moment is enlightenment. The Buddha made the claim that worshiping things outside of yourself can be harmful. He said, "The way is not in the sky. The way is in the heart." What we are looking for is within us. That is the truth.

The Buddha was a revolutionary figure who challenged the traditional spirituality of his day. He challenged adherence to dogma and the authority of religious leaders. He wanted us to know that we could be our own religious leaders. He said, "Believe nothing unless it agrees with your own understanding and common sense." In a way he was a populist religious teacher, saying that we should be in charge of our own religious destiny instead of being followers. The Buddha taught that we should always think for ourselves and always question everything. This is an important lesson and it really separates him from other spiritual teachers.

I AM ENLIGHTENED AND SO ARE YOU

Enlightenment really consists of recognizing the Buddha nature that is within us already. Our Buddha nature is our true self. It's the self that is one with everything and realizes that fact. It's the self that is fully enlightened and perfect. In reality, it's who we are right now, even if we don't realize it.

It's not some goal to be achieved—each and every one of us is enlightened already. We just have to awaken to that fact. We just have to conquer the delusions that prevent us from realizing the fundamental truth of our being. It's not an easy goal, but there are special methods and practices that are designed to help us on the path. Few choose to be on the path and many give up.

When we have enlightening experiences that help us start to recognize our true nature, they help us stay motivated to remain on the path. As long as we don't forget and become deluded again, the motivation will remain present.

Buddha nature is a key concept in Mahayana Buddhism. It simply means that we are all enlightened already. It is just because we are suffering from delusion that we don't realize it. We don't think of enlightenment as something to be achieved, like a trophy. If we contemplate this deeply, it is very significant.

I am enlightened and so are you. Stop and think about that for a minute.

If I am enlightened already, then I can celebrate my success right now. I certainly don't need to feel bad about not getting enlightened sooner. If I am enlightened already, then the Buddhist path doesn't seem nearly as daunting. If all I am doing is clearing away delusion, that seems a lot more achievable than getting some high spiritual goal.

My kids are interested in Buddhism and they get very excited about the whole thing. Meditating, chanting mantras, and listening to dharma talks are very exciting to them. They inspire me to want to be a better Buddhist.

And they make me ask the question: why aren't we more excited about Buddhist practice?

They don't say, "Om mani padme hum"—they shout it. Children yell Buddhist mantras because they get excited. And they should be excited. The Avalokiteshvara mantra is supposed to awaken great compassion within us. That should be exciting.

So why aren't people more excited? I can't answer that, but I think they should be. I think we can be excited about Buddhism, especially if we have confidence and faith. Not faith in something 'out there' that will help us—faith in ourselves. Our delusions are deep seated and difficult to remove. But our true nature is enlightened already, so there is a reason to have confidence in our ability. We just have to put in the work. We have to

67

take steps to awaken ourselves through the paths of conduct, insight, and concentration. These three things are very important to the path.

How do we unleash our Buddha nature? Our main tool for this is meditation. Our minds are full of constant distraction. Our true nature is right there for us to recognize, but we don't because our minds keep us deluded with nonstop mental chatter and noise. We get caught in our ego, which falls into the delusion that we aren't enlightened very easily. We meditate to deal with this.

Meditation is a method of quieting the mind, of getting the mind to the point 'before thought,' where we are just observing what's going on instead of getting caught up in distracting thoughts. When we meditate we can start to bring our awareness to our true nature.

A daily meditation practice is recommended. Just 20 or 30 minutes a day. As we start to meditate, we will realize that we are one with everything. Our delusions will slowly start to be stripped away. We will become better people naturally.

If we try to act as though we are enlightened already, that helps. It's easier to meditate when we are kind to others. It's also easier to clear away delusion. Selfishness and anger cause us to accumulate more delusion, so working hard to manage these negative emotions is very helpful too.

Meditation is the cornerstone of Buddhist practice. We can have an intellectual understanding of Buddha nature and other spiritual concepts, but it's meditation that allows us to actually experience it. Without meditation, we aren't really experiencing anything.

Knowledge without experience is not what Buddhism is about. Buddhism is not so much a belief system as a path. It is more something we do than something we believe. Meditation is the most crucial tool to clearing away our delusions and unleashing our Buddha nature.

ON TAKING REFUGE

We call the process of becoming Buddhist 'taking refuge in the Triple Gem'. We rely on the Triple Gem to guide us in our spiritual journey and to show us the right way to liberation.

The Triple Gem has three components: The Buddha, The Dharma, and the Sangha.

The Buddha is the teacher and example for us. It is because of looking at his example that we know that awakening is possible.

The Dharma is the list of teachings that the Buddha and later teachers have delivered to us. It is through studying and practicing these teachings that we are able to walk the Buddhist path.

The Sangha is the spiritual community. I am a part of the Sangha I meditate with, but I am also part of the worldwide Buddhist community. We walk the path together.

Buddhist Sutras usually mention a few basic ways that taking refuge helps us on the path.

1) When we take refuge we become students of the Buddha. He is our teacher and we are connected to him through the refuge we have taken.

2) We will improve our characters a great deal. The act of taking refuge automatically improves our cultivation of morality because we have made a commitment.

3) Those of us who take refuge will have the opportunity to meet many good people. We are part

of all of the global Buddhist community and because we've taken refuge in the Sangha we know that we aren't in this alone.

4) When we take refuge we lay the foundation for further spiritual growth. This act leads on the path to Enlightenment. When we take refuge we are planting the seeds for our own awakening. We are taking the first step to unleashing our Buddha Nature.

THE REVOLUTIONARY NATURE OF THE 4 NOBLE TRUTHS

I think we take the four noble truths for granted in the Buddhist community.

These truths are one of the first things you learn when you begin to study Buddhism. It seems like a simple concept at first, but if we contemplate it deeply, we can discover that it is more revolutionary than we initially suspect.

We can hear the four noble truths and repeat them over and over, but to truly understand them is a different thing entirely.

The first noble truth is that all of life is suffering.

This seems pretty easy to understand. We are all acutely aware that there is a lot of pain in life, and that things aren't always good. So, on the surface, the first noble truth seems like an idea that should be easy for us to accept.

Although we can accept that there is suffering in life, we may tend to expect the pain in life to go away some day. In our culture, we often think that if we work hard enough or if we think positively enough, the pain and suffering in our life will disappear. But from a Buddhist perspective, this belief doesn't hold up under scrutiny.

We can't avoid the pain of life. At the very least, no matter how good things are, we are still going to get sick and grow old. We are still going to see the people we care about grow old and die. This is a fact of life, and this fact is pain that we can't escape.

The goal of Buddhism is to escape suffering. I want to be clear that pain isn't necessarily the same thing as suffering. Pain is something that is a universal part of life; we can feel pain without making ourselves suffer over it. I sometimes think of it this way.

Pain is inevitable, but suffering is something that we consciously choose and control.

We compound every problem in life by suffering over it. We often worry about things that are not in our control, and this worry only makes it worse.

Getting angry about things doesn't help either. Buddha said, "Getting angry at someone is like grasping a hot coal to throw it at them. You are the one who gets burned."

Getting angry only makes us unhappy. It doesn't help the situation, but often worsens it. When we have an irritating problem, we have to worry about our own irritation as well as the problem. It would be much easier to just focus on the problem.

When we are stressed out, we tend to amplify any negative situation that happens to us. For example, if I am frustrated because I can't find the t.v. remote and I happen to stub my toe while I'm looking for it, that stubbed toe is going to hurt a lot worse than it would have without the initial frustration of searching for the remote. It is going to make me mad at everything. If we are already stressed out, then even a very minor thing can add to our suffering a great deal more than it should.

The second noble truth is that the cause of suffering is craving/attachment.

That might be a slightly more revolutionary idea than the first noble truth. In other words, you can't always get what you want. Yet, we tend to think that we can. By this, I don't mean to say that everyone is optimistic—I know that is not the case.

78

Most of us don't go around thinking we will suddenly become millionaires or be surrounded by supermodels asking for our love. But there are many people who feel that they should get what they want simply because they want it. If I want the perfect job, for example, I could develop a sense of entitlement, and believe that because I want it, the world should provide it. This entitlement could make me feel bitter if I don't get the job. This can be a source of unhappiness and make our suffering much greater.

It is especially dangerous if this entitlement is coupled with a belief that we should not have to try very hard to get what we want. That might be part of what the Buddha intended when he revealed the first noble truth. When he said that life is full of suffering, maybe it was a response to the people who think that one day life may not be full of suffering. It's a deeply rooted belief that things should go our way and that if they do, our pain will be over.

79

The first noble truth explains to us that pain is a natural part of life.

Even when some part of our life seems to be perfect, it doesn't last forever. We hope it does, and we often cling to the things we want for fear of losing them. We so desperately want things to last forever, but nothing ever does.]

Everything is impermanent.

It makes little difference if the change happens because we lost something or because our attitude has changed and we don't really want it anymore. And, once we have what we really think we want, it often ends up not nearly as perfect as we pictured it.

We are very imaginative. We can come with all sorts of fantasies about what it will be like when we have this cool car or that hot girlfriend.

80

I think, to a certain extent, society encourages these fantasies. That's why celebrity worship is so popular these days; it's easy for us to wish that we could be one of the rich and talented famous people that we worship. We wrongly believe that they don't suffer like we do.

If we acknowledge that they suffer too, then wishing we were them isn't nearly as appealing.

Nothing can be as wonderful as it is in our fantasies. I think that's why rock stars often seem to end up ruining their lives with drugs and other kinds of reckless behavior. This can happen when people are so motivated to 'have it all,' and when they get to the top, they realize they still lack perfect happiness. They still suffer just like the rest of us. They don't know where to go next because they achieved all of their goals. What can you do when you're at the top, and you're still unhappy?

Our culture doesn't help; from an early age, society

conditions us on our perception of happiness. We learn that getting what we want will make us happy. We learn the myth of living happily ever after.

It's an unfortunate fact of life that when we have everything, the truth is that we still have nothing. Everyone suffers from attachment and nothing is ever perfect. It's always going to be that way. This sounds negative, but it's the truth. That's another reason why the four noble truths is a revolutionary concept.

When we believe the four noble truths, we are facing the harsh facts about reality. We are not trying to hide from the truth behind a delusion that at some point our lives will be without pain. I think that on some fundamental level we do realize that. Our Buddha nature knows the truth, and when we start to unleash it, the truth becomes more evident.

There is no perfect life. We might wish for it, but it isn't real—life is full of suffering because we crave things.

But, there is hope. People sometimes think that Buddhism is very negative because of the four noble truths. That might be why there is not as much excitement towards Buddhism as there is in some other spiritual paths. But, it's not wholly negative.

The third noble truth is that there is a way out of suffering.

We can pretend that our pain isn't real or that life can be perfect at some point, but this kind of thinking is not helpful. I think it's better to understand the facts about reality. Only then can we experience personal and spiritual growth.

It's like having a terminal illness. Most of us, I think, would rather know that we have a terminal illness than be kept in the dark about it. Knowing the truth is a good thing. We must accept the first two noble truths to relieve our suffering.

Beneath our suffering is something very positive, it's there for us to access. We are one with everything. The core of our being is there.

When oneness with everything can be experienced, pain is a lot easier to handle.

Our ego causes our suffering. If we are attached to the idea that we have a fixed independent self, then we will suffer a great deal. If we can look beyond our limited self, then we can escape from suffering.

There is still a reason to have hope, in spite of the fact that life is full of suffering.

The fourth noble truth is the way out of suffering.

We get out of suffering by transforming ourselves.

It is the noble eightfold path; this is the path that leads to enlightenment. It is what gives us hope for freedom from suffering; that's the ultimate point of the four noble truths. Although life is full of suffering, there is a way out.

Pain is unavoidable but suffering is something that we can escape.

If we follow the path the Buddha set out for us we can lessen our suffering. The Buddha said, "I do not teach religion. I only teach suffering and the end of suffering."

If we just follow the eightfold path of Right Understanding, Right Thought, Right Speech, Right Action, Right Livelihood, Right Effort, Right Mindfulness and Right Concentration, we can overcome our suffering.

IS ALL OF LIFE SUFFERING?

The Buddha taught the four noble truths. Briefly: All of life is suffering, The cause of suffering is attachment, there is a way out of suffer, and the way out of suffering is the eightfold path.

The First Noble Truth is essentially the foundation of all of Buddhist philosophy, so it's worth scrutinizing further.

The Buddha said, "All that I teach is suffering and the way out of suffering."

Sounds like more of a life coach than religious teacher, doesn't he?

I've heard these questions:

Is all of life really suffering? Can that be true? Isn't that a really negative way of looking at life?

I don't know if you've met a lot of Buddhists...we don't tend to look at life in a really negative way.

"All of life is suffering" does sound really negative. It makes it sound like Buddhists are all weird goth kids who sit around writing bad poetry about how sad they are or something. But this is not the case.

Obviously plenty of things in life are not suffering. Hearing my children laugh, having my cat come sit with me when I meditate, making love. All of these things are clearly not suffering. There are plenty of moments in life that are not full of suffering.

So, what's the deal? Did the Buddha tell us something that's only partly true? Is the foundation of Buddhism shaky?

Suffering is a partially adequate word for it, of course. The connotations involve things not going the way we want them to, life not meeting our expectations. Suffering, in this context, represents not the pain of life, but the way our minds sometimes tend to make things worse. If I lose my keys, that's a problem, but if I start to get stressed out and frantic about the fact that I lost my keys, that makes the problem much worse than it was initially. That is what is meant by life is suffering. A better way to put it might be, "we have a tendency to exacerbate our suffering." and the Buddha taught, "How to stop exacerbating our suffering." But that seems really long.

We have to remember an important thing. The Buddha didn't use the word, "suffering." He couldn't have. He didn't speak English. He spoke a language called Pali. The word he used was Dukkha. We only use the word suffering because that was the original translation the first time someone translated a Buddhist text into English.

So, what does dukkha mean? It's been translated as suffering, or stressful, or unsatisfactory.

To me those terms have the same problem.

What does dukkha really mean? It has several connotations in the original language. It can mean suffering but it can also mean always changing, and it can also mean impermanent.

Imagine if the original translation was "all of life is change" instead of "all of life is suffering."

Things change all the time, many things change that we wish wouldn't. Some change is good and some is bad, but change happens whether we like it or not. And people do struggle with this. It's the most obvious in the way that people try to avoid aging.

Aging is a sure sign of impermanence. As we get older, we have a constant reminder that things are always changing. Some people handle it well and some don't.

Do change and impermanence relate to suffering? Obviously they do. We lose things we want to keep forever, up to and including our youth and our health.

I would translate it as "life will never be perfect" instead of "life is suffering" if I had to. We sometimes think that if our life is a certain way we will finally stop suffering. That's not really how the world works, but it's an intellectual trap that we can easily fall into.

I humbly suggest that we stop using the word suffering. There are some words that are difficult to translate, words for which we just use the original terms. Dharma, Sangha, Karma, Buddha, we've decided to use these words instead of English equivalents because it's simply too hard to adequately convey their meaning in translation.

 I think dukkha should be added to this list because when we say, "all of life is suffering," that can easily give people the wrong idea.

The four noble truths seem simple at first, but really understanding them is difficult.

EXCAVATION

Meditation practice is like digging.

Through the process of silent illumination we are digging through levels of delusion that are accumulating in our hearts and minds. This is like a spiritual excavation.

These layers involve our delusions and the preconceptions that shape our view of reality. These layers also involve our tendency to bifurcate reality, to think in terms of 'self' and 'other' or 'this' and 'that'. r o

Some of what we are digging through are acquired delusions and preconceptions. Some are innate, affecting all human beings.

If we can dig through these layers, then we can see the empty mind ground. This is sometimes called 'no mind' or 'beginner's mind' or 'mind before thought'.

This is said to be ultimate reality, the way things are before we start labeling and categorizing and judging things.

Because of our layers of delusion, sometimes instead of knowing what's really going on, we get caught up in our labels and judgments about the situation. We can spend a lot of time locked in our delusions, not seeing reality.

But we can do something about this. Enlightenment is the goal of Buddhist practice. A healing of our delusion. An excavation into our minds to discover the jewel of our true natures.

So, I sit on the cushion in silent illumination. This is my shovel. There are other tools available, like chanting or koan practice, but silent illumination is the tool I choose to use.

I see a layer of greed and I dig through it, pushing

away the dirt that has collected. I want many things.

Then I see a layer of aversion and I dig through that too, sweeping away the dirt and grime that's collected there. There are many things that I DO NOT want there.

Then I see a layer of delusion. That's the hardest one to penetrate. The labels and categories I put things in are arbitrary and create many distractions.

So start digging.

MEDITATION IS ALSO BIOHACKING

The concept of biohacking is slowly becoming more well known. Similar to computer hacking, it's the idea that our biology is like a program, something that we can constantly tinker with and improve. There are many different forms and they involve thinking outside the box in regards to self improvement. They include things like alternative diets, alternative learning methods, and putting strange things into your body. Biohacking also involves alternate ways of working with our minds.

I bring this up here because I think of meditation as a form of biohacking, possibly one of the oldest forms of biohacking.

There are those that think that meditation brings us to some natural state of peace. I respectfully disagree with that idea.

There is list of things that meditation helps improve. The mindfulness that we gain from meditation helps us deal with anxiety, fears, stress, selfishness, etc.

These are things that have been evolutionary successful to us in the past. In the modern world, getting eaten by a tiger isn't really a concern for me, so I don't really need to have as much anxiety and fear as my ancestors. It simply isn't as helpful.

So, the Buddha was a biohacker. He saw how his mind worked, how much his own mind caused him to suffer and he figured out a way to do something about it. He didn't invent meditation. It's a practice that has existed much longer than Buddhism. But, he refined it. He gave it a new context and he did start working with mindfulness in new ways.

Meditation is mind hacking because it helps us to

understand the world around us a little better. Sometimes we need to help ourselves put things in context.

More importantly, meditation helps us understand our own minds a lot better. It's hard for my mind to understand my mind. It takes a hacker to do that. It takes thinking outside the box.

4:30 AM

Some People Think I'm Crazy for Getting Up at
4:30 Every Morning to Meditate Before Work.

Those People are Right.

My alarm (which is my phone) goes off and I roll
out of bed in the dark. I exit the bedroom holding
my phone, trying not to wake up my wife while cats
are trying to get by me and enter the room.

My morning routine starts with going to the
bathroom. After that, it's time for meditation. I grab
my cushion and put in on the floor in my meditation
spot. I sit on it in the half lotus position and
meditate for thirty minutes, using my phone as a
timer.

Then I go shower, get dressed, and eat breakfast.
Then I pack my lunch and go to work.

I have to get up at 4:30 to do this. If I don't, I simply
don't have time. My shift starts at 6:00. One of the
things about meditation is that if I don't have plenty
of time then I feel like I have to rush. And that
feeling is definitely not conducive to a good
meditation practice.

There's a certain calm and quiet to 4:30 in the
morning. The world isn't awake yet. I have two
small children and obviously they aren't awake at
4:30. It's the only time when my house isn't loud. I
do a short meditation before bed every night, but
once in a while I have to skip that one because the
kids are struggling with bedtime.

I never have to skip my 4:30 meditation.

COMMIT TO SIT

I need to have a stronger commitment to my meditation practice. I think we all do.

Meditation is hard. That seems counter-intuitive. Just sitting and doing nothing, counting our breaths? That should be easy. It should be just about the laziest thing in the world. And people love to be lazy, don't they?

But it isn't easy. Why? Well, I think it's because it seems like the world is conspiring to stop us. We have so many ways to entertain and occupy ourselves.

It can be hard to just sit when we're too busy thinking about watching tv or playing a video game or messing with our cell phones or goofing around on facebook. Our culture teaches us that we have some sort of right to be entertained ALL THE TIME. Not only do we have the right to this, we sometimes feel like we have to. I don't think that's a natural part of the human condition. I think that's something we've learned. We have learned to not be mindful and we have to figure out how to get past it.

Although today when I was meditating, I got distracted because I started thinking about writing this.

The Buddha talked about the five hindrances, a list of five things that tend to get in the way of meditation practice. They are: Desire, Ill will, sloth, restlessness, and doubt.

1. Desire

If we can just rearrange the circumstances of our lives, we will finally be able to be happy. That's it, in a nutshell. Our desires can easily get us off track. We are endlessly distracted by them. How often do we neglect the things we need to do because of the cravings and desires that we have? Pretty often.

Attention is how we counter this hindrance. When we realize intellectually that our desires are not helping us, we can control them. It's not about not having desires, becoming emotionless robots. It's about controlling our desires, not letting them run away with us. Of course we want things. Our lives are uncomfortable. It's just that we don't want our desires to carry us away.

2. Ill Will

This represents an intense feeling of emotional pain in unpleasant situations. Feelings of resentment, hostility, hatred, and bitterness stem from this hindrance. Some aversion is good, but when it turns us really hostile it becomes a problem. It's not that we should like everything, it's just that our relationship to the things we like shouldn't be damaging us so much.

3. Restlessness

This represents anxiety. I can't do this. I am worried. I want to stop. This is when we know what we should be doing, but we have the jitters. It's obvious how this would be a hindrance to meditation. It's hard to quiet the mind while sitting when what I really want to do is get up and move around. But, this applies in daily life too. When I'm at work sometimes I've just been staring at that computer screen too long and I just want to get up and walk around instead of staying focused. This is the hindrance of restlessness.

4. Sloth

This represents boredom. I could be doing something fun. We tend to expect the world to entertain us, especially in the modern world. Why should I be bored when I could be browsing the internet with my phone or watching Netflix? A dedicated daily meditation practice is a little hard to maintain sometimes, especially at first. It's hard to do nothing when I have so much that I could be doing. This can be a hindrance in daily life too because we sometimes tend to put off things that we need to get done because they're boring. I think this really applies to housework and things like that.

5. Doubt

This represents a lack of belief in ourselves. If I think I'm not good

enough, then I am suffering from the
hindrance of doubt. Don't use doubt as
a reason to not improve yourself. This
applies to any kind of self-
improvement. It's the 'can't win, don't
try' attitude.

~

These hindrances usually come up in life. No one is
perfect. Being aware of them is the first step to
overcoming them.

UNLEASH YOUR BUDDHA NATURE!

Enlightenment consists, really, of recognizing the Buddha nature that is within you. Your Buddha nature is your true self. It's your self that is one with everything and realizes that fact. It's your self that is fully enlightened and perfect. And, in reality, it's who you are right now, you just don't realize it. It's not some goal to be achieved. Each and every one of us is fully enlightened already. We just have to awaken to that fact. We just have to conquer the delusions that prevent us from realizing the fundamental truth of our being. It's not an easy goal, but there are special methods and practices that are designed to help us on the path. Few choose to be on the path and many give up.

When we have enlightening experiences that help us start to recognize our true nature, they help us stay motivated to remain on the path. As long as we don't forget and become deluded again, the motivation will remain present.

Buddha nature is a key concept in Mahayana and
Vajrayana Buddhism. It simply means that we are
all enlightened already. It is just because we are
suffering from delusion that we don't realize it. We
don't think of enlightenment as something to be
achieved, like a trophy. If we contemplate this
deeply, it is very significant. I am enlightened and
so are you. Stop and think about that for a minute.

If I am enlightened already, then I can celebrate my
success right now. I certainly don't need to feel bad
about not getting enlightened sooner. If I am
enlightened already, then the Buddhist path doesn't
seem nearly as daunting. If all I am doing is
clearing away delusion, that seems a lot more
achievable than getting some high spiritual goal.

But our true nature is enlightened already, so there
is a reason to have confidence in our ability. We
just have to put in the work. We have to take steps
to awaken ourselves through the paths of conduct,
insight, and concentration. These three things are

very important to the path.

How do we unleash our Buddha nature? Our main
tool for this is meditation. Our minds are full of
constant distraction. Our true nature is right there
for us to recognize, but we don't because our minds
keep us deluded with nonstop mental chatter and
noise. We get caught in our ego, which falls into the
delusion that we aren't enlightened very easily. We
meditate to deal with this. Meditation is a method of
quieting the mind, of getting the mind to the point
'before thought', where we are just observing what's
going on instead of getting caught up in distracting
thoughts. When we meditate, we can start to bring
our awareness to our true nature.

Daily meditation practice is what is recommended.
Just twenty or thirty minutes a day. As we start to
meditate we will realize that we are one with
everything. Our delusions will slowly start to be
stripped away. We will become better people
naturally. If we try to act as though we are
enlightened already, that helps. And it's easier to

meditate when we are kind to others. It's also easier to clear away delusion. Selfishness and anger cause us to accumulate more delusion, so working hard to manage these negative emotions is very helpful too.

Meditation is the cornerstone of Buddhist practice. We can have an intellectual understanding of Buddha nature and other spiritual concepts, but it's meditation that allows us to actually experience it. Without meditation we aren't really experiencing anything. Knowledge without experience isn't what Buddhism is about. Buddhism is not so much a belief system as a path. It is more something we do than something we believe. Meditation is the most crucial tool to clearing away our delusions and unleashing our Buddha nature

THE FOUR IMMEASURABLES

The Brahmaviharas, or Four Immeasureables, are a list of four Buddhist virtues that we can cultivate through our meditation practice. They are considered antidotes to negative mental states.

Although this list of virtues has it's origin in Buddhism, it would probably work equally well in any religious tradition. The Four Immeasurables are sometimes discussed as virtues in texts of Jainism and Hinduism. But they are Buddhist in origin (we think).

The Four Immeasureables are: Loving-kindness, Compassion, Joy, and Equanimity.

Loving-kindness is the wish that others be happy. That sounds easy, but it is supposed to include everyone, not just our friends and people we know, but everyone. When we cultivate loving-kindness, we are trying to extend it, first to all the people we love, then to the people we feel neutral about, then to the people we dislike/hate. Only when we can really cultivate this can it be said to reach the Immeasurable level. Loving-kindness counters ill will.

Compassion is similar. It is the wish for others to be free from suffering. Again, we want to cultivate compassion and try to extend to include all beings, not just the ones who we love, or who we think 'deserve' it. Wishing suffering upon others or turning a blind eye to it is not helpful to us. It can plant negative seeds in our minds. Compassion counters cruelty.

Joy is the attitude of rejoicing at the happiness and virtues of other sentient beings. Again, we want to cultivate joy and try to extend it to all beings. When others are happy, we want to take joy in this. This is the counter to jealousy.

114

Equanimity is the attitude of regarding all beings as equals, regardless of their relationship to oneself. This sounds simple, but it's probably the hardest to cultivate. It involves trying to view all things as equal, not being attached to our circumstances or to our desires. Letting things just be as they are. Equanimity counters clinging and aversion.

OUR INTELLECT IS PART OF THE PROBLEM

The intellect is part of our problem. This reminds me of that old saying, "You need to get out of your own way." It's a cliche, but I think it's really relevant to this discussion. Our minds are our greatest strength but also our greatest weakness.

The intellect is the seat of our trouble because it's the source of all of our ignorance and distractions. When we are thinking about the future or the past instead of focusing on what we are doing, that is our intellect causing trouble.

If we can act without letting our intellect distract us, then that is helpful. I experience this when I don't get enough sleep because I'm too busy thinking about the past or the future and I can't relax. I definitely experience this when I'm trying to meditate. Constant discursive thinking makes meditation incredibly difficult.

The Diamond Sutra, one of my favorite Buddhist texts, teaches us that we need to focus on disciplining our minds, to help with the trouble our intellect causes for us. The Buddha said to Subhuti, "all the Bodhisattva Heroes should discipline their minds." This is a very important message. Peace is within and we achieve it by disciplining our minds. We practice meditation in order to train our minds. Later in the sutra, the Buddha says, "All Bodhisattvas, lesser and great, should develop a pure, lucid mind."

It is our minds that trap us in the delusions of ego and dualism. The Buddha makes it clear that ego is a delusion when he says, "Though the common people accept egoity as real, the Tathagata declares that ego is not different from nonego."

It's important to remember that our egotism, our belief that we are separate from everything else, is delusional. The truth is that there is no dualism. All things are connected. It can be easy to fall into the delusion of dualistic thinking, even during our Buddhist practice, and it is something we need to

118

watch out for. That is the great danger that our intellect presents.

DANIEL SCHARPENBURG

THE SIX PERFECTIONS

The six perfections are: generosity, virtue, patience, diligence, concentration, and wisdom

The Perfection of Generosity

The perfection of generosity represents more than just giving material things. Obviously it does represent giving money or items to the needy. It also represents giving your time, things like helping a friend move or spending time comforting someone who is suffering from a loss. We can also give someone less tangible things, like our love, respect, or patience. We can also offer stability, being reliable. If we make plans with someone and keep those plans, we are giving them stability. We can also give someone space when they want to be alone, or quiet when they are being bothered by too much noise.

The practice of generosity is beneficial to us. It increases our confidence and self-esteem. It also helps lessen our attachments. If we give material things, it helps us lessen our attachment to material things. Cultivating generosity is helpful in developing love, joy, and compassion.

The Perfection of Virtue.

This perfection represents ethical behavior, morality, self-discipline, integrity, and nonviolence. The essence of this perfection is that through our love and compassion we do not harm others. We are devoted to being virtuous in our thoughts, speech, and actions. This practice of ethical conduct is an important aspect of our path.

We abstain from killing, stealing, lying, divisive speech, harsh speech, gossip, and greed. We follow this path so that we can enjoy greater freedom, happiness, and security in our lives, because through our virtuous behavior we are no longer creating suffering for ourselves and others. We must realize that unethical behavior is always the cause of suffering and unhappiness. Practicing the perfection of virtue, we are free of negativity, we cause no harm to others by our actions, our speech is kind and compassionate, and our thoughts are free of anger. When our commitment is strong in the perfection of virtue we naturally become more positive.

The Perfection of Patience.

This perfection is the enlightened quality of patience, tolerance, forbearance, and acceptance. The essence of this perfection of patience is the strength of mind and heart that enables us to face the challenges and difficulties of life without losing our composure and inner tranquility. We embrace and forbear adversity, insult, distress, and the wrongs of others with patience and tolerance, free of resentment, irritation, emotional reactivity, or retaliation.

We cultivate the ability to be loving and compassionate in the face of criticism, misunderstanding, or aggression. The ability to endure, to have forbearance, is an important part of the path. In practicing this perfection of patience and forbearance, we never give up on or abandon others—we help them cross over the sea of suffering. We maintain our inner peace, calmness, and equanimity under all circumstances, having enduring patience and tolerance for ourselves and others. With the strength of patience, we maintain our effort and enthusiasm in our Dharma practice.

The Perfection of Diligence

The fourth perfection is diligence. It involves continuing to persevere when the path is difficult. It includes right effort, enthusiasm, and the energy needed to overcome unwholesome thoughts and attitudes as well as the cultivation of positive virtues, study of Dharma and the choice of right actions.

Diligence requires eagerness and sharp interest ipurge path. It requires active bodily or mental strength to improve our personality for individual enlightenment and supreme Buddhahood for the sake of all sentient beings. We need the energy of diligence to stay on the path.

When we are on the right path, we will be diligent in studying ourselves, in seeing the true reality, and in having the sustained energy needed to attain

124

Buddhahood. Through diligence we can generate great compassion to help others and ourselves.

The Perfection of Concentration

This perfection represents concentration, meditation, contemplation, and mental stability. Our minds have the tendency to be very distracted and restless, always moving from one thought or feeling to another. This can cause us to be heavily attached to our thoughts and emotions. The perfection of concentration means training our mind so that it does what we want it to. We stabilize our mind and emotions by striving to be mindful and aware in everything we do. When we train our minds in this way we achieve focus, composure, and tranquility. Concentration allows the deep insight needed to challenge our delusions and attachments that cause confusion and suffering. This development of concentration requires diligence. In addition, when there is no practice of meditation and concentration, we cannot achieve the other perfections, because their essence, which is the inner awareness that comes from meditation, is lacking. To attain wisdom, compassion, and enlightenment, it is essential that we develop the mind through concentration, meditation, and mindfulness.

The Perfection of Wisdom

This perfection is the enlightened quality of transcendental wisdom, insight, and the perfection of understanding. The essence of this perfection is the supreme wisdom, the highest understanding that living beings can attain, beyond words and completely free from the limitation of mere ideas, concepts, or intellectual knowledge. The Perfection of Wisdom is the supreme wisdom that knows emptiness and the interconnectedness of all things. The Perfection of Wisdom is a result of contemplation, meditation, and rightly understanding the nature of reality. The sixth paramita is what truly ties the other five together and is often considered the most important.

In a way, the Perfection of Wisdom is the sum of the other five perfections. If one is able cultivate generosity, patience, virtue, diligence, and concentration, this will naturally lead to the cultivation of wisdom. Wisdom represents an awareness of the truth of our nature. It is our intuition, our innate understanding that everything is interconnected, that we are one with everything. Just as a wave in the ocean is never really separate from the water although for a time it appears to be, so are we. We are all waves and the universe is our ocean. When we act in accordance with this fact, then we are dwelling in nirvana. Recognizing our interconnectedness is unleashing our Buddha Nature. We have this wisdom already, we just have to clear away the delusion and unleash it.

BEDTIME MEDITATION CLUB

It all started when my wife started working nights.
It was a temporary job, not intended to last more
than a few months, but it was a period of adjustment
for us. I became in charge of dinner, evening
activities, and bedtime. Before mom had been the
sole ruler of these things, as is probably true in a lot
of households.

It wasn't a big change. We believe in actively
sharing the parenting duties, so I'm used to doing
lots of things with the kids.

One night after bedtime, my son James (age 4)
came out of his room and caught me meditating by
the front door.

Some explanation is necessary. For the past ten
years I've been a morning meditator. I am the rare

person who loves getting up early in the morning, so I'm up before everyone else and I enjoy a great deal of peace and quiet in my house before anyone gets up. This has always been the perfect time for me to meditate.

But, in recent months, I had added meditating before bed. I had been wanting to add another meditation style to me practice of following the breath, and I thought the easiest way to do that would be to add more meditation. This practice, by the way, is called 'hua tou', or "what's this?" meditation.

So, I would put the kids to bed and go grab my meditation cushion and go sit by the door and meditate every night.

When my son James came out and caught me meditating, his sister Nissa (age 7) was already asleep. She's an early riser, like me. James is a crazy person at night, like his mother.

James came out of his room and just looked at me as I sat facing the wall. Without a word, he went back to his room and returned with a pillow.

He placed his pillow right next to my cushion and faced the wall as well. We sat there in silence for the rest of my meditation practice, nine minutes.

Anyone that has meditated with children knows that nine minutes is a pretty big accomplishment, especially with a three year old. But James did it.

Then he asked me, "Dad, what's this?"

And I replied, "Meditating."

"Me like 'editating," he said with a smile.

I laughed.

The next night, as I was getting ready to put the kids to bed, James said, "Dad, we have to 'editate! We can't go to bed."

I laughed.

"What did he say?" Nissa asked.

"We meditated together last night," I replied.

As James grabbed his pillow and headed for the wall, Nissa grabbed one too.

Now, I should point out, I lead a Buddhist Sunday School every Sunday. I know that my daughter does not like meditation. She's really into chanting and

Buddhist stories and yoga, but she is not a fan of sitting still and being quiet.

So, I thought she probably just didn't want to feel excluded. Or perhaps seeing that a three year old boy can meditate is really good inspiration for anyone to take the practice more seriously.

I set a timer for fifteen minutes and gave a little instruction.

"Just follow your breath. Every time a thought arises, just bring your attention back to the breath," I said.

And we sat there in silence for fifteen minutes. Neither child got restless or distracted. We just meditated.

This was the beginning of our Bedtime Meditation Club.

WHEN BUDDHA SAID HE WASN'T A FAN OF RELIGION

There is an old story called the Kalama Sutra. It is one of the oldest sutras and one of my favorites.

It goes something like this. The Buddha was traveling the world spreading the Dharma, teaching people that wanted to listen. He came upon a group of people known as the Kalamas and started explaining the Dharma to them. Their response was unusual.

They said, "We have had numerous spiritual teachers come here. Every new teacher comes and tells us to ignore the teachings we have heard before and to follow their doctrine only. This has made us doubtful and uncertain. What makes your teaching different? Why should we follow your authority and not the authority of the other teachers?"

The Buddha's reply was unique.

He said, "It's good to be skeptical, to doubt, to be uncertain; uncertainty has arisen in you about what is doubtful. Don't believe things just because you've heard them from rumors or from authority figures or scriptures. Even if something has been repeated for generations, that doesn't mean we shouldn't challenge it. We should challenge everything. You should even challenge what I tell you. But challenge your own preconceptions too.

You didn't need a religious teacher to come tell you that greed, hatred and delusion are bad. Your common sense agrees with that. You didn't need a religious teacher to come and tell you that compassion and mindfulness are good. Your common sense agrees with that too.

I have only really come to teach skillful means, methods to deal with the suffering that pervades our lives. If my teachings are right, then the truth is within you already. Other teachings may be dogmatic and strict. Mine is not. I only teach suggestions for dealing with suffering."

This is an important message in my opinion. I have a natural inclination to both be skeptical and to challenge authority. Unlike many other religious teachers, that is actually what the Buddha suggests to us.

In my opinion he wasn't really trying to start a

religion at all, he was just providing an example for us to follow, more of a way of life than a religion.

IKKYU, ZEN REBEL

An Iconoclastic Monk: Enlightenment Through
Real Living

> "The autumn breeze of a
> single night of love is better
> than a hundred thousand
> years of sitting meditation."
> ~Ikkyu

Ikkyu was an eccentric iconoclastic Zen monk and poet in the 1400s.

Ikkyu Sojun was the embodiment of iconoclastic Buddhism.

Raised in a Rinzai Zen monastery, he was an illegitimate son of the emperor of Japan—so his mother put him in the monastery to make sure he would be safe.

The Buddhism he learned was strict and had a rigid hierarchy.

Ikkyu really loved the Dharma, but he was not a fan

of the hierarchy. He felt that it was political, which the Dharma should not be. So when he reached adulthood and they offered him the certificate of enlightenment that would allow him to become a fully ordained Zen Monk, he refused. He left the monastery instead.

He thought that the monks he met were just acting spiritual and focusing on the hierarchy instead of the Dharma. Some believed that enlightenment could only be found by breathing in incense and sitting in silent meditation for hours at a time. Ikkyu disagreed. He believed enlightenment was with us already and we could realize it just as easily by spending our time with poor people and prostitutes as we could with monks. So that's what he did.

He became a wandering monk and was given the nickname 'Crazy Cloud'.

The point of Ikkyu's life story is that the 'sacred' is nothing more than ordinary life experienced with mindfulness. His view was non-dualistic. He traveled the country doing things that we don't associate with monks. There are a lot of stories about him traveling the country, drinking sake, and sleeping with women. He was freedom-loving and he didn't really care what the religious authorities of the time thought.

Instead of staying in monasteries like most monks, Ikkyu gave teachings in places monks didn't usually go. He taught in the streets and in brothels. His students were hobos, criminals and prostitutes. A lot more of his students were laypeople than monks because he thought the Dharma was for everyone.

He created his own version of Zen. He called it Far Out Zen. He thought that Zen should be life affirming and positive. He didn't believe that the renunciation that many monks practiced was helpful. He had a great passion for life and said that we should too.

But, at the same time, he expected a lot from his students. His ways taught that having a regular meditation practice was important.

His students were dedicated to Buddhist practice, but in the context of secular life, in the real world instead of in monasteries.

Far Out Zen was radical in its non-dualism. This

version of Buddhism includes the entire world in its teaching, rather than being confined to sacred spaces. If all beings have Buddha nature, then enlightenment isn't a matter of lifestyle, it's a living experience. When his teachers tried to get him to stay in a monastery, he wouldn't do it. He wanted to be in the world, working for the Dharma.

Is this bad? I think his story is a lesson. We shouldn't be attached to what we think a good Buddhist should do and we certainly shouldn't be attached to systems of authority. Good and bad are just labels. More than that, challenges to authority are important, especially religious forms of authority. Even if you think Ikkyu was wrong in his iconoclasm, it's important that he was there to make the challenges.

Is there Far Out Zen today?

No. Ikkyu didn't name a successor, so he didn't create a lineage. Rinzai Zen is still around, but the offshoot that Ikkyu created died with him. But, many in the Zen tradition do revere him today. It's sad that he didn't preserve his lineage, but he was probably concerned that after his death it might become another sect like the ones he had rebelled against.

Maybe we can try to practice Far Out Zen anyway.

What do you think?

THE MEANING OF CH'AN BUDDHISM

The Ch'an ideogram first appeared in China around the same time that Buddhism arrived, around 100 AD. It's believed to be a translation of the Sanskrit word 'dhyana'. 'Dhyana' is usually translated as 'meditation' in English. Dhyana is a spiritual practice that involves using the mind to transform the mind.

The ideogram didn't exist before this time. There were plenty of teachings regarding mind development in China, Confucianism in particular had a very developed teaching of mind development that involved the cultivation of inner peace through studying classic texts. However, there was nothing quite like the meditation teachings of Ch'an. When the concept was brought to China, a new word had to be created.

The creation of the Ch'an ideogram can be said to represent the process of assimilation of the idea of 'dhyana' into Chinese culture. Although the Dharma is, in essence, beyond cultures and nationalities the Chinese might have seen it as a foreign practice. So, the concepts were transformed in way that allowed

145

not only Buddhist ideas to enter China, but also Chinese ideas to enter Buddhism, flowing back to India.

When we practice Ch'an, we are cultivating five positive qualities that can counteract the five hindrances. These are: Directed Thought, Evaluation, Rapture, Pleasure, and Oneness of Preoccupation.

Directed Thought is used to counteract Sloth. Evaluation is used to counteract Doubt. Rapture is used to counteract Hatred, Pleasure is used to counteract Anxiety, Oneness is used to counteract Sensation desire.

This is the essence of the Ch'an method. This is how we can begin to understand the Empty Mind Ground. It's not something we are seeking to find or achieve, but rather something that is with us already. Enlightenment is already within our minds.

All of the different skilful means, such as hua tou and kung an practice, have the goal of realizing emptiness and perceiving the Empty Mind Ground. This is what the Buddha meant when he talked about Enlightenment. It is awakening to our true nature. To perceive the Empty Mind Ground is to become one with it intuitively. Although Ch'an tradition stays away from distinctions like 'this' and 'that' or 'enlightened' and 'unenlightened', the ideogram implies a duality.

示

This is the left particle of the Ch'an ideogram. It represents a person kneeling at a shrine. This had a certain meaning in China at the time. Shrines and altars often represented things like shamanistic spirituality and Confucian influence. So, in its original form, the shrine represented the worshiping of one's ancestors. Confucianism also had a method for training the mind, but it involved scholarly study instead of seated meditation. The study of the Confucian classics is a method for cultivating mindfulness, but it's a form that is completely different from seated meditation.

In this case the altar is transformed. The altar is given a new meaning and becomes timeless. It represents our self cultivation on the path. It is the doorway through which the teachings came to China, not as 'Indian' teachings, but as acultural teachings. Although we aren't worshiping something outside of ourselves, we are engaged in spiritual transformation. Because of this, an altar is a good simple to represent our path.

單

This is the right particle of the Ch'an ideogram. This symbol has two distinct meanings. The first meaning is that of a net, as would have been used to catch animals. This represents our effort to catch our deluded thoughts. In the second meaning it represents a single person in isolation. This represents the solitary act of meditation. This is important because meditation is the core of the oldest Buddhist teachings. Some branches of Buddhism place emphasis on studying scriptures and chanting endlessly, but the oldest Buddhist teachings are those that rely heavily on seated meditation.

This is significant, of course, because the Buddha didn't attain Enlightenment because of reading a sutra. He attained Enlightenment because of meditation. Not that sutras aren't helpful, but there can be a tendency to become so attached to studying sutras that we study in lieu of actually practicing.

This is also significant in the context of the isolation meaning. Many spiritual practices involve practicing with others. Even the scholarly study of Confucians involves engaging with the author of whatever text one is reading. Meditation involves only looking within yourself. Even when we are in the meditation hall with others, we are not interacting with them, we are isolating ourselves and looking within. It should be noted that Ch'an includes many things in addition to meditation methods. The uniqueness of Ch'an involves interaction with a Ch'an master.

Ch'an masters taught with a variety of methods. But, the Ch'an ideogram does seem to be a good representative of the Buddhism that first arrived in China, before it fully evolved into the Ch'an that we know today.

Taken together:

礻單

The Ch'an ideogram represents a spiritual activity, often carried out in isolation, that involves the gathering of scattered thoughts through one-pointed concentration, symbolized by a net. This is a very accurate representation of the early Buddhism that arrived in China. Meditation is the core of early Buddhism and so that was what the creators of the

Ch'an ideogram thought of when they were creating it.

Although Ch'an was a concept so foreign to the first students of Bodhidharma in China, the influence did go both ways. While Ch'an Buddhism influenced Chinese culture, it was also shaped by it. As Ch'an moved through other countries to become Zen in Japan, Son in Korea, and Thien in Vietnam, ultimately coming to the west, it retained its Chinese influence. The reason we know it as Zen in America is because the Japanese version is the one that first successfully planted itself in America.

Ch'an was heavily influenced by Taoist schools of thought that were common in China at the time. The line from the Diamond Sutra that is said to have caused the Enlightenment of the sixth Patriarch Huineng, "Let your mind function freely without abiding anywhere or in anything." sounds very similar to the Taoist notion of "flowing like a river."

It's also a big similarity that Ch'an and Taoism both suggest to use that the truth remains 'outside the scriptures'. Not something we can get from others, but something we have to perceive ourselves. It's for this reason that studying with a teacher who actually knows you is thought of as a more successful path than studying sutras. Sutras can only take you so far. But then, your teacher can only take you so far too, ultimately the message is that we must walk the path ourselves.

It could be this Taoist influence that separates Ch'an from other branches of Buddhism, making it unique. It has been argued by some Ch'an teachers that Ch'an represents a combination between the original Vipassana meditation as taught by the Buddha and Taoism. I think that is a pretty accurate description. It would be difficult to try to remove the Chinese influence from Ch'an Buddhism.

Our methods include several forms of meditation, some study of words of the ancient masters, and interacting with a teacher.

I'm a true believe. I think our true nature exists under layers of delusion. Because it's our true nature to be Enlightened, we can find it. It can come upon us all at once.

Huineng, the 6th Ch'an Patriarch, was an illiterate woodcutter. He heard someone reciting a text called the Diamond Sutra and he suddenly entered the stream. After that, he found a Ch'an teacher and started cultivating the seed of Enlightenment. This is the authentic spiritual journey that many people have gone through. It exists throughout history.

The purpose of Ch'an is Enlightenment, self realization, awakening to the absolute truth of reality.

It's a path of transformation instead of salvation.

We have a constructed image in our minds of who we are and what the world is. Ch'an is about being in the moment without the constructs. Dropping ego. Dropping the past and our thoughts about the future and engaging with the present moment. Zen Master Dogen called it "The dropping away of body and mind"

Easier said than done. Our minds want to do anything but stay in this moment. Ch'an involves learning to quiet our minds and penetrate through these layers of delusion. Ch'an is teaching our minds how to sit still so we can perceive our true nature.

Any discussion of Ch'an history has to involve Bodhidharma. The story of Ch'an says that it comes from the Buddha, the historical founder of

Buddhism. The story says that he passed Ch'an teachings to one of his followers and it was passed from teacher to student for many many years. There's not a lot of historical evidence for this. But that's okay. What we do know is that it has been taught from teacher to student since around 400ad. The purpose of the teacher is both to set an example and to provide context for us for what's happening as we progress along the path.

Enlightenment is available all the time because it is our true nature.

Our true nature is one with everything and the only reason we don't see that is because we are in layers of delusion. When we meditate we clear some of that delusion. We have to dig ourselves out.

We train to realize our true nature. We investigate ourselves.

We just have to be present to perceive our true nature.

The path has been handed down for centuries. In the early days it only consisted of transmission from one teacher to one student. They practiced together and over time the teacher would ask questions to help the student untie knots in their mind. Teachers would teach students to lay down thoughts and when the teacher could see a level of attainment, they would give dharma transmission, permission to teach and spread the dharma.

This changed over time. Teachers started taking many students and giving transmission multiple times. That's not bad. We probably wouldn't be here right now if that hadn't happened.

Today there are lineages and organizations and schools. Many of them are very different. Lineages teach in their own style. Some require monasticism. Some, like the one I am in, discourage it. Ch'an has been evolving in different ways for hundreds of years.

THE THREE ESSENTIALS

These are considered some of the greatest and most important virtues.

They are great faith, great doubt, and great determination.

Great faith means having faith in our mind's ability to recognize our Buddha Nature. This is clearly very different from what other religions usually mean when they suggest that we should have faith. In Zen Buddhism faith means faith in yourself. It is holding on to the belief that the Buddha nature is present within us.

Great doubt is like the scientific method. It means don't believe in anything unless we can demonstrate the truth for ourselves. All of our beliefs should be examined and re-examined often. Beliefs should be accepted or rejected based on our judgment. Any ideas that are found to be unhelpful, should be rejected.

In Ch'an we do not follow our religious teachers and

leaders blindly. We check every belief against our own knowledge and experience.

It's about having a healthy amount of skepticism. It might seem like great doubt and great faith are at odds.

The truth is we need a healthy dose of skepticism to temper our faith in ourselves.

Great determination is a firm resolution to go forward in our practice. It's about staying on the path and avoiding discouragement. It's about cultivating patience and self-discipline.

Zen is not always easy and it's important to remember that there are no shortcuts.

These are important virtues in life and we should cultivate them.

THE LEGENDARY LEGEND OF BODHIDHARMA

Huike said to Bodhidharma, "My mind is anxious. Please pacify it."

Bodhidharma replied, "Bring me your mind, and I will pacify it."

Huike said, "Although I've sought it, I cannot find it."

"There," Bodhidharma replied, "I have pacified your mind."

In the 5th century he appeared in China. Sources differ on whether he came from India or Persia. He has been described as a blue eyed barbarian with a giant beard. We only know him from his Buddhist name, Bodhidharma.

He is credited with bringing not only Ch'an Buddhism to China, but also the martial art that would come to be known as Shaolin Kung Fu. His

157

life story is full of wild myths and legends.

When he arrived in China, he was already famous.
Word had spread that this great Buddhist teacher
was coming, so everyone was ready for him. I
picture it like the papparazzi waiting for a celebrity.

There are many legendary stories about
Bodhidharma that are probably mythical.

It's said that he spent nine years in a cave
meditating non-stop. They say that Bodhidharma
invented tea to help him stay awake during hours
and hours of meditation.

One story involved Bodhidharma meeting Wu, the
emperor of China. The emperor of China was a big
fan of Buddhism and he wanted to meet this
famous, already legendary, teacher. They had a
dialogue that went like this:

Emperor Wu: "How much merit have I gained for

ordaining Buddhist monks, building monasteries, having sutras copied, and commissioning Buddha images?"

Bodhidharma: "None. Good deeds done with worldly intent bring good karma, but no merit."

Emperor Wu: "So what is the highest meaning of noble truth?"

Bodhidharma: "There is no noble truth, there is only void."

Emperor Wu: "Then, who is standing before me?"

Bodhidharma: "I know not, Your Majesty."

This is the teaching style of Bodhidharma. He challenged preconceptions at every opportunity. The emperor tried to meet with Bodhidharma later, but he refused.

Here's another story.

There was a man named Huike who wanted to learn from Bodhidharma. He went to the cave that Bodhidharma was living in and requested to become his student. Bodhidharma refused, telling him to go away.

Huike didn't give up. He stood outside
Bodhidharma's cave in the middle of winter,
waiting for Bodhidharma to change his mind. He
stood until snow was up to his waist.

In the morning, Bodhidharma asked Huike what he
wanted and Huike said, "I want a teacher to open
the gate of the elixir of universal compassion to
liberate all beings".

Bodhidharma refused, saying, "how can you hope
for true religion with little virtue, little wisdom, a
shallow heart, and an arrogant mind? It would just
be a waste of effort."

This reminds me of the scene in the film Fight Club,
when Brad Pitt refuses the first applicant to their
little terrorist house and the guy just waits outside
for days until they let him in. I wonder if that scene
was inspired by the story of Huike.

Anyway, in an incident that's more hardcore than a Brad Pitt movie, after waiting a long time, Huike demonstrated his determination by cutting off his own arm. Bodhidharma was impressed by his commitment and accepted Huike as his student, eventually making him his heir.

Is this story true? I doubt it. But, it doesn't matter. The point is we should be determined to practice. We don't have to make the level of sacrifice that Huike did, however.

Bodhidharma met the monks at a monastery called Shaolin and he thought they looked out of shape. So, he invented Kung Fu so that they would get some exercise.

Bodhidharma's teaching was pretty simple and straightforward. He said we should be focused on practice, rather than giving too much faith to religious texts. The concept that enlightenment is with us already comes from Bodhidharma.

He described Ch'an as:

"A special transmission outside the scriptures,

Not founded upon words and letters;

By pointing directly to [one's] mind

It lets one see into [one's own true] nature and [thus] attain Buddhahood."

And he was a big advocate of a style of meditation that he referred to as 'wall-gazing'. This is the style of sitting meditation in which we sit facing a blank wall, keeping our eyes open, and attempt to quiet our minds. No visualization, no chanting, just silent meditation.It's my favorite style of meditation.

Many of the branches of Buddhism have different rituals and things going on. Bodhidharma's buddhism did not. Direct and to the point was how he wanted it.

BODHIDHARMA'S TWO ENTRIES

Bodhidharma said that there are really only two ways to enter the path. They are entry through conduct and entry through principle. He outlined this in a teaching called the Two Entries and the Four Practices. In this teaching he outlines in a clear way what we must do to attain enlightenment. Entry through conduct is associated with practices that need to be done. This applies to those aspects of our training that require effort, our spiritual cultivation. Entry through principle is considered the essence of the Ch'an path. It applies to directly seeing our true nature, which is beyond words, descriptions, and forms.

In the practice of the Dharma, both of these things need to be used. Entry through principle represents the cultivation of insight through meditation. Entry through conduct represents the cultivation of discipline.

Entry through Conduct is the path of the Dharma as it's explained in the sutras and commentaries. It is an approach that involves modifying behavior and spiritual cultivation, in which concentration is expanded through meditative practices. It also involves efforts at countering the three poisons: hatred, greed, and delusion.

Entry through conduct is practiced through four methods:

1) The practice of repaying wrongs.
2) The practice of adjusting to circumstance.
3) The practice of non-seeking or asking for anything.
4) The practice of upholding the Dharma.

Repaying wrongs represents understanding that our actions have consequences and trying to mitigate negative consequences that we have caused. This has been described as karma. Our karma has to be understood and improved.

Adjusting to circumstance means doing our best within whatever environment we find ourselves in. Accepting our conditions instead of becoming attached to them is important. Attachment to our circumstances can be either positive or negative. We can enjoy our circumstances too much and be too excited by them. We can also hate our circumstances too much and view life in a very negative way. These are two sides of attachment.

Non-seeking means acting without attachment to personal gain either now or in the future. The self is a delusion, a label we put on our interaction with our environment. If we act in a way that is attached

164

to receiving praise or blame, this is not helpful. In a
way this could be said to be an advanced practice.
Many people come to Buddhism with hope for a
gain, for some kind of benefit from practice. But,
eventually when one practices, self-centeredness
does start to fall way. When we are concerned about
our Enlightenment, it can be a barrier to our
Enlightenment. Wanting to achieve some attainment
can stop us from perceiving the Empty Mind
Ground.

The Practice of Upholding the Dharma represents
our attempt to perceive the emptiness and
impermanence. This is our practice that allows us
to reach the point of Entry through principle.
Different branches of Buddhism have different
methods of engaging this practice. In Ch'an the
method involves meditation but also interaction
with a Ch'an teacher.

Altering our behavior in this way is supposed to
calm our minds and bring us to a point at which we
can perceive the Empty Mind Ground.

Entry through principle is a different method that
Bodhidharma taught. It represents an insight into
our true nature. It is a method for touching the
Empty Mind Ground right now and it is difficult for
us to understand on an intellectual level.

Bodhidharma said: "When conveying the tradition of enlightenment, it is understood that all beings – whether enlightened or unenlightened - share exactly the same true nature. However, the Buddha-nature is obscured by a layer of dust which prevents the 'real' from manifesting. Give-up delusion and return to the real by concentrating (and stilling) the mind so that it is broad, and all inclusive. Then there is no self or other, and there is no difference between a sage and an ordinary person. Firm and unmoving, there is no falling into the written teachings. This deep realisation is in accord with the principle. There is no discrimination, and all is silent and non-active."

This is the most important principle of Ch'an, as it was taught by Bodhidharma. The enlightened state is our true nature. We have delusions that are preventing us from realizing that, but if we can just get past those then we can enter the Empty Mind Ground. This means leaving behind our delusions and our discrimination between self and other.

These two entries are the foundation of the Ch'an School in China.

HUINENG, ILLITERATE MONK

Huineng is one of the most influential
teachers in the history of Zen Buddhism. He
lived in the 600s in China, before Zen
spread out to the rest of Asia. The two
schools of Zen that exist today, Rinzai and
Soto, were created by his successors. He's
so beloved and respected today that's it's
almost hard for us to believe that he was a
hated rebel in his time. He challenged
conventional thinking about enlightenment.

Huineng was poor. His father died when he was
very young and his family never really recovered.
He never had time to learn how to read or write. He
made a meager income selling firewood.
The story says that one day he overheard someone
reciting the Diamond Sutra and he instantly became
enlightened. He immediately left his life behind and
sought out a famous Buddhist teacher named
Hongren.
Huineng was allowed to live in Hongren's mountain

monastery, but he wasn't allowed to become a monk. He was considered to ignorant and poor. It's said that he looked like a barbarian. So, he was like a janitor. He did chores around the monastery. This is when the story sounds just like the film 'Good Will Hunting'. Ever since I saw that movie I picture Huineng as Matt Damon and Hongren as Stellan Skarsgard...

Hongren was looking for a successor, someone to take his place. He challenged the monks that lived there, of which there were many, to compose a verse that effectively explains the true essence of the mind. Whoever could successfully do this, would be his successor.

A student named Shenxiu wrote the following verse:

The body is a bodhi tree / the mind a mirror bright / At all times polish it diligently / and let no dust alight.

He wrote this on the wall in the middle of the night so every would see it when they got up in the morning. It sounds pretty good, right? Clear your minds, be enlightened.

The other monks in the monastery were so
impressed by Shenxiu's answer that they didn't
even try.

But, when Huineng asked someone to read it to him
and he heard it he wasn't impressed. There wasn't
really anything bold or new about it. Huineng had
another worker help him write his own verse on the
wall next to Shenxiu that night. It said:

  Bodhi is fundamentally without any tree; /   The
bright mirror is also not a stand. / Fundamentally
there is not a single thing —
  Where could any dust be attracted?

In Buddhism we learn that the way the think about
ourselves is fundamentally incorrect. Individuality
is an illusion. We are all interconnected to
everything and we don't really have a separate 'self'
that we can describe in any serious way. Huineng is
attacking Shenxiu's answer, which was the

traditional zen answer of the time, as shallow and meaningless. Shenxiu says, "You must purify yourself." and Huineng replies, "There's no self there to purify."

This is a really heavy concept. Sit with it for a minute if you need to.

Hongren took Huineng to his room and read this from the Diamond Sutra: "use the mind, but be free from any attachment." And in that moment, Huineng was fully enlightened and he exclaimed: "How amazing that the self nature is originally pure! How amazing that the self nature is unborn and undying! How amazing that the self nature is inherently complete! How amazing that the self nature neither moves nor stays! How amazing that all dharmas come from this self nature!"

We are enlightened already. Huineng's story is a big reminder that anyone can be enlightened at any time because it's our true nature. We just have to unleash it. It's also important because sometimes we get discouraged.

Remember kids, if an illiterate janitor can become enlightened, you can too.

Shenxiu and some of the other monks were unhappy about all of this. They wondered how this poor barbarian janitor could possibly be the new zen master.

Shenxiu actually said, "screw this, let's start our own zen, a better zen!" It didn't work out for him. Shenxiu's lineage of students did not survive. All Zen lineages today trace their roots back to Huineng, the illiterate monk.

DANIEL SCHARPENBURG

PANG, ENLIGHTENED DAD

"My daily activities are not unusual,

I'm just naturally in harmony with them.

Grasping nothing, discarding nothing.

In every place there's no hindrance, no conflict.

My supernatural power and marvelous activity:

Drawing water and chopping wood."

Layman P'ang is considered a model for the potential for non-monastic Buddhists to reach their full potential. He lived in the 700s. He was a bureaucrat, working for the Chinese government. He got married and had two children, a daughter and then a son. One day, he just grew to become interested in spiritual matters. He built a little hermitage on his property and started spending time retreating there with his kids and meditating. His daughter Ling-chao was especially interested in the Dharma and studied it with him throughout his life.

P'ang studied with a Ch'an teacher named Sekito in a monastery called Nan-yueh for a year. Sekito put him through monk training, but ultimately P'ang refused to become a monk. He left the monastery.

There is a famous dialogue between P'ang and Sekito.

Sekito asked, "How have you practiced Ch'an since coming here?"

and P'ang replied, "My daily activities."

P'ang traveled to a place called Kiangsi and studied with an even more famous Zen teacher named Baso. Once again, after studying for a year, Baso offered to make P'ang a monk. Again, P'ang refused. He didn't want to be part of a hierarchy. He was a lot happier practicing Buddhism with his family and challenging the norm.

Becoming a monk was considered normal. He was unwilling to allow joining a Ch'an hierarchy to restrict his options. He wanted to live in a way that was open and free, not bound by the constraints of the system. He spent his time wandering from place to place, discussing spirituality with any who would listen. He spent as much time talking about the Dharma with the homeless and the working class as he did with monks and scholars.. Free of monastic rules and hierarchical duties, we was able to challenge the best and brightest minds of his day.

He also wrote a great deal of poetry. Here's a poem

he wrote:

"Well versed in the Buddha way, I go the non-Way.

Without abandoning my ordinary man's affairs,

The conditioned name-and-form are all flowers in the sky. Nameless and formless, I leave birth and death."

Layman P'ang is one of my favorite Ch'an teachers. He was nervous about following authority figures so he made his own way. The Dharma doesn't have to adhere to a strict hierarchy. Sometimes people become far too attached to tradition and customs and forget to focus on the Dharma at all. The Dharma is beyond such things. P'ang rebelled against the notion that he had to become a monk in order to spread the Dharma. In spite of being such a radical figure, and he really was quite radical in his day, he is beloved and revered today.

Also, he practiced Buddhism with his children. I really connect with that. Like him, I have a son and a daughter. They are very interested in being involved in my practice with me as well. So, Layman P'ang is one of my heroes. Maybe I just love anyone who is willing to challenge authority.

DANIEL SCHARPENBURG

178

DOGEN

I think it could be argued that the history of Zen is really a history of spiritual iconoclasts and revolutionaries, spiritual adventurers who saw the way things were and sought to innovate instead of merely accepting the status quo.

Dogen is looked upon by Soto Zen Buddhists as an ideal to live up to; he represents everything that Soto Zen is and is thought of as mainstream.

But, in the beginning, he was a radical. He saw the Buddhism that had arrived in Japan and he found it lacking. So, he traveled to China to see what else he could learn—and he came back and started the Soto Zen sect.

Dogen quickly learned the meaning of the word impermanence—while still young, he lost both his parents. So, he was inspired to study Buddhism.

I've always felt a special connection to Dogen because losing my parents is what inspired me as

179

well.

Dogen was an illegitimate child in a noble family and became an orphan at an early age and he became a monk at Mount Hiei, a Tendai Buddhist monastery.

Later in life, he had this to say about his time there: "They maintain that all beings are endowed with Dharma-nature by birth. If this is the case, why did the Buddhas of all ages find it necessary to seek enlightenment and engage in spiritual practice?"

This is significant. Dogen is considered a hero now. But he was, like many historical Zen Buddhists, someone who constantly asked questions. We need to learn this lesson—the Buddha told us to investigate thoroughly.

As a young monk, he was questioning Buddha nature, a very well known Mahayana teaching. He found no satisfactory answer to his question. He asked several Tendai teachers and one of them suggested that he travel to China and study Ch'an Buddhism.

In China, Dogen went to several leading Ch'an monasteries. At the time, most Ch'an teachers relied heavily on the use of gong-ans (koans). A simple description would be these are riddle-like phrases that are supposed to shock the student into having some sort of realization.

Dogen studied these gong-ans, but he didn't understand why so much emphasis was placed on them. He found them to be a little bit useful, but only to a certain point. He wondered why there wasn't more emphasis on sitting meditation and sutra study.

He was offered Dharma transmission and he turned it down. He wasn't happy with the teachings, so he rejected the teacher's approval. He wanted to find a lineage that was more in line with his views. He didn't want Dharma transmission from a teacher that disappointed him.

After Dogen had been in China for two years, he heard about a Ch'an master who had a different style of teaching.

Rujing was a teacher in the Caodong School of Ch'an. Dogen traveled to Mount Tiantong to meet him.

Rujing told Dogen to "Cast off body and mind."
Dogen said that this was when he became enlightened. The simple hearing of that sentence gave him an awakening experience.

Dogen described Enlightenment this way:
To study the Way is to study the Self. To study the Self is to forget the self. To forget the self is to be enlightened by all things of the universe. To be enlightened by all things of the universe is to cast off the body and mind of the self as well as those of others. Even the traces of enlightenment are wiped out, and life with traceless enlightenment goes on forever and ever."

Rujing's teaching was based on sitting meditation and Dogen really connected with it. This was a big change from some of the other Buddhist teachers he had met. There are even some lineages in Zen today that hardly meditate at all, focusing almost entirely on gong-an practice.

A few years later, Dogen received Dharma transmission from Rujing; Dogen returned to Japan after seven years in China.

He wrote down a text called the "Fukan Zazengi" and distributed it; it was a set of instructions for sitting meditation and emphasized why sitting meditation is important.

He brought the philosophy he had learned to Japan, naming it 'Soto' Zen and created his own temple called Eihei-ji.

He was a prolific teacher and writer. He composed a long text called the 'Shobogenzo' that is considered one of the most important works in the Zen tradition.

He died at the age of 53, after giving Dharma transmission to one of his students. Soto Zen grew a great deal and Dogen's legacy has been a great influence on Japanese Buddhism.

Dogen's Main Teachings:

Dogen repeatedly emphasized the importance of 'zazen' or sitting meditation. He said that meditation is the core of Zen practice and study. He taught it to both monks and the laity, saying that everyone should learn it. This is a departure from some teachers in the past who had said that these teachings should only be available for monks and nuns.

This is what he wrote about it:

> "For zazen, a quiet room is
> suitable. Eat and drink
> moderately. Cast aside all
> involvements and cease all
> affairs. Do not think good
> or bad. Do not administer
> pros and cons. Cease all the
> movements of the
> conscious mind, the
> gauging of all thoughts and
> views. Have no designs on
> becoming a Buddha. Zazen
> has nothing whatever to do
> with sitting or lying down."

He described zazen and enlightenment as one. Sometimes we might feel like our meditation is unproductive. Dogen is telling us that that's not the case, that Enlightenment is right here for us to get. This is important because when we think of

Enlightenment as something 'out there' that can be harmful to our spiritual practice. It can cause us to look outside of ourselves instead of within.
He said:

> "To practice the Way singleheartedly is, in itself, enlightenment. There is no gap between practice and enlightenment or zazen and daily life."

THE FIERCE ZEN OF SUZUKI SHOSAN

The Samurai who became a monk.

> "To learn to be always in a state of meditation means never to let your vital energy wane. You would never allow it to do so if it were certain that you were to die tomorrow." `
> ~Suzuki Shosan

In Japan in the 1600s, a well known samurai retired at the age of 40 because he wanted to learn Zen.

He served under Shogun Tokugawa Ieyasu and it wasn't until right after a decisive victory that he asked to be released from his samurai duties.

The Shogun allowed it.

He decided to live the life of a wandering monk. He traveled around Japan studying under different Zen masters. He spent a lot of time studying Zen history and he was really inspired by the stories about a certain iconoclastic Zen teacher from a couple centuries earlier named Ikkyu.

Although he spent a great deal of time studying with a teacher named Daigu Sochiko, he never received Dharma Transmission.

Suzuki Shosan declared himself Enlightened. And he didn't even change his name to a Buddhist name.

Now, this might sounds scandalous: self-declared Enlightenemnt? Surely that couldn't happen then or now!

Well, it did. It actually wasn't all that rare at that time. (It happens now too!) Here in the West we sometimes think of Dharma Transmission as something really special. And it is, or it's supposed to be.

But during Suzuki Shosan's time the Zen community was very political. There was a thing going on that is sometimes called "Temple Transmission."

That's when someone is given Dharma Transmission, declared an Enlightened Master, for political or expedient reasons. It was one of the things that Shosan's hero Ikkyu had condemned in the Zen establishment.

Example: Zen Master X needs someone to head a certain temple because the previous head of the temple has died or left. Zen Master X wants the head of the temple to have Dharma Transmission. So, he gives a student Dharma Transmission. Zen Master X didn't wait until a student was Enlightened, he waited until he needed a student with Dharma Transmission around.

Not only that, but some temples were known to give Dharma Transmission for money, the same way diploma mills sell PhD s today. We don't like to admit it, but this kind of thing happened.

The Dharma Transmission system is great. It has served us very well. But it's not perfect. Because nothing that involves human beings can be perfect. Not only that, but most Zen temples were, to a greater or lesser degree, connected to the Japanese government, which could be good sometimes and bad at other times.

Sometimes it seems like Zen history has two tracks.

Temple Zen is full of monks that live in monasteries and chant and meditate and memorize sutras all day.

Renegade Zen is full of people that challenged the establishment, that thought of things in new ways, that weren't afraid to innovate.

The renegades: Dogen, Rinzai, Ikkyu, Huineng... these are the ones that we remember. There is an iconoclastic current at work here.

Anyway, Suzuki Shosan declared his own Enlightenment because he didn't want to deal with politics.

(No, I'm not going to do that. Thanks for asking.)

At this time in Japan this happened sometimes. He was not unique. Although he didn't bother with the temple system for certifying his Enlightenment, he also didn't go around criticizing the temple system. I think that's an important point.

Anyway, even though he wasn't a 'good' Zen Master, I still think his teaching can be useful to us.

He taught something that he called Nio Zen. The Nio are those scary looking figures that stand outside of some Zen temples in Japan.

They are supposed to be these demon guardians that protect the Dharma.

Shosan told his students to visualize the Nio in meditation, to help them channel energy and vitality. He believed that the fierceness of the Nio could help us conquer the three poisons.

He also told his students to be ready for death at any moment, as a way to strengthen present moment awareness. This, it is thought, was inspired by his career as a samurai.

But this is why I really like him: There was a pretty popular view in Shosan's time that to attain Enlightenment, one had to separate from the world. If not actually become a monk, at least spend a lot of time alone. Shosan didn't believe that. He thought that the message of

Enlightenment could and should be brought to everyone at all levels of society. If Buddha nature is our true nature, then anyone should be able to attain Enlightenment, from the most high level monk down to the lowly criminal. Although he lived the life of a monk, he specifically told people that they didn't need to, that Enlightenment was already available right here in this moment.

Suzuki Shosan built 32 Zen temples, which is in itself and incredible achievement.

He was 76 years old when he died.

He left behind a book of teachings called "Parting the Grasses at the Foot of the Mountain."

He wasn't a 'good' Zen Master, but I like him. He was more worthy of the title than many people who receive it in the official way.

XU YUN

Ch'an Master Xu Yun lived to be 120. He lived from the 1840s until the 1950s. He never traveled to the West. But many westerners traveled to the East to learn from him.

As a child, he saw monks performing a funeral service for his grandmother. Seeing these monks gave him inspiration. He started tracking down and reading sutras and he fell in love with the Dharma.

At the age of 19 he ran away from home to become a monk. It's hard for us to even conceive of living for 120 years, let alone spending 101 of those years as a monastic.

His teachings helped Ch'an Buddhism survive into the modern age. He is given credit for keeping Ch'an alive and breathing new life into it through his dynamic teachings. Students of his, such as Sheng Yi and Charles Luk, have done a lot to bring his version of Ch'an teaching into the modern world.

Xu Yun's philosophy is heavily characterized by three things. One, he was a strong user of the Hua tou method of meditation. Two, he was known for giving the same amount of respect to layman as to monks. He said that layman were as capable of attaining Enlightenment as monks. Three, he talked about Enlightenment. In many Buddhist traditions, discussing the actual experience of Enlightenment is frowned upon. Master Xu Yun wanted to guide people to perceiving the Empty Mind ground and he didn't think there was a problem with talking about it in simple and direct ways.

He actually described his own experience of Enlightenment with two gathas:

"1 - A cup fell to the ground
With a sound clearly heard.

194

As space was pulverised,
The mad mind came to a stop.

2 - When the hand released its hold, the cup fell and
was shattered,
'Tis hard to talk when the family breaks up or
someone dies.
Spring comes with fragrant flowers exuberating
everywhere;
Mountains, rivers and the great earth are only the
Tathagata."

From his Enlightenment at the age of 54 until his
death, Xu Yun traveled around the countryside
teaching sutras, transmitting the precepts, building
temples, and starting seminaries for novices,
Buddhist associations for lay men and free Buddhist
schools for children.

In the 1930s, when he was in his 90s, Xu

Yun decided that spreading Ch'an to the West

was a good idea. So, he asked his lay student

Charles Luk, to translate as many Ch'an

teachings into English as possible. Charles

Luk was very prolific in these translations and many of them are available online.

A lot of the Japanese style, Zen, has come to the West. Quite a bit of the Korean style, Son, has come to the West as well. But very little of the original Ch'an Buddhism has come.

As a result of his long life and lack of scandals, Xu Yun is revered in China and is slowly becoming known in the West. He spent his life rebuilding temples across China and visiting other Buddhist teachers. It is thought that Chinese Buddhism might have died out without his century of work preserving it. Thanks to Master Xu Yun, a transmission of Chinese Buddhist teaching has spread from China out into the rest of the world. Thanks to Master Xu Yun, there are authentic Ch'an lineages that are growing.

WE ALL WANT TO CHANGE THE WORLD. IT STARTS WITH YOU

We all want to change the world. It starts with you.

Look deeply within yourself. We tend to think that we don't create our identity, but that's not true. We constantly create and re-create it. Look within yourself and find the preconceptions and thoughts that aren't helping anyone and try to let them go. Sometimes this can be very difficult, but if we really want to understand why we do and feel the things we do, the answer is within us. We CAN improve ourselves. The only person you should try to be better than is the person that you were yesterday. Through meditation we can understand our minds a little better. Our minds are full of preconceived ideas and we sometimes don't even know it. That's why we can do things like make snap judgements, or be angry at

199

someone when they haven't even done anything yet, or be sad because our life hasn't changed fast enough in the way that we want it to change. Preconceived ideas are often harmful.

And we can improve society as well. I don't think people realize how many of the things that divide us are arbitrary and manmade. Religion, Political Views, Money, even Race. Humans invented these because we like to put things in categories. That doesn't make the categories real. It's hard to wrap our heads around the difference between REALITY and our conception of reality. I can say "my phone is black." But that's not really true. Black is just a label I've put on it to make things easier for myself. Labels and categories can be helpful, but when they're not we need to try to let them go.

BONES OF THE BUDDHA STATUE

Once Ikkyu was staying in a temple. The night was very cold and there were three wooden Buddhas in the temple, so he burned one Buddha to warm himself. The priest in charge of the temple woke up and noticed something was going on, so he looked to see what Ikkyu was doing.

The Buddha statue was burning and Ikkyu was sitting there warming his hands over the fire.

The priest got angry. He said, "What are you doing? Are you a madman? — and I thought you to be a Buddhist monk, that's why I allowed you to stay in the temple. And you have done the most sacrilegious act."

Ikkyu said, "But the Buddha within me was feeling very cold. So it was a question whether to sacrifice the living Buddha to the wooden one, or to sacrifice the wooden one to the living one. And I decided for life."

The priest was so angry that he couldn't listen. He said, "You are a madman. You simply get out of here! You have burned Buddha."

So Ikkyu started to poke the burned Buddha with a stick. There were ashes, the Buddha was almost consumed by the fire. .

The priest asked, "What are you doing?"
Ikkyu said, "I am trying to find the bones of Buddha."

So the priest laughed and said, "You are either a fool or a madman. And you are absolutely mad! You cannot find bones there, because it is just a wooden Buddha."

Ikkyu laughed, he said, "Then bring the other two.

The night is still very cold and the morning is still far away. I haven't burned the Buddha. I've burned a wooden statue. And you called me the crazy one."

What can we take from this? Is it just a funny story? Maybe.

I think it represents iconoclasm. The priest is, in a sense, worshiping this Buddha statue. We shouldn't worship it. We shouldn't worship anything, really, but we especially shouldn't be attached to an icon.

When we give a statue of the Buddha that much respect we are doing what the Buddha said not to do. He said that the Dharma is what really matters, not him.

Historically it seems that the Buddha rejected the Guru/disciple teaching method. He often said, "You should think for yourselves." And I think that is important to remember.

After his death, many branches of Buddhism did adopt the Guru/disciple method. They would probably do well to read stories like this one.

AFTERWORD

BUDDHA IN THE LAND OF THE PAGANS

I went to a pagan hippie camp to teach about meditation practice. In the spirit of my hero Ikkyu, of course I was willing to go anywhere that involved people that wanted to hear about the Dharma, especially places where other Dharma teachers were unlikely to go.

Ikkyu went to bars and whorehouses and homeless camps to spread the dharma. The least I could do to try to uphold his legacy is go to places like hippie campgrounds.

This is my journal of the experience. If it reads differently than the rest of the book, that would be why. It is completely autobiographical. I brought them the teachings, but I learned a lot from the people and the land as well.

As this is my journal, it is completely honest and authentic and I have changed none of the details, in spite of the fact that a few of the details might be embarrassing. I've done very little editing. Sorry if it's choppy in some parts.

I included all of the details of the teachings I gave, so there is some good basic Buddhism information here.

I, along with my wife and four year old son, entered the Heartland Pagan Festival and traveled to another dimension.

I was there to teach meditation and other Buddhist practices in a hippie pagan camp—because I will give the Dharma to anyone that wants it, and a friend asked me nicely. And because I'd rather be

206

teaching the Dharma to people that aren't as boring as I am, sitting around endlessly chanting sutras like many Buddhist teachers.

I believe in going to places where other meditation teachers aren't going. Places like campgrounds and the street are my temples.

In the beginning I was a tourist, a visitor to this bizarre place. By the end I had just about assimilated completely.

I was full of anticipation when I left work at 2:30 p.m. on Thursday and went home to get Wendi and James. We had done most, but not all of the work loading the car the night before. We loaded the car and drove.

Gaea Retreat Center is located in a rural area of Kansas and is designed to be a cultural and spiritual retreat center for a variety of spiritual and cultural groups. We were invited to this event called the Heartland Pagan Festival. I was given free tickets and meals for myself and my family. I just had to teach two workshops. One on meditation and one on the teachings of the Buddha. We arrived around 6:00 p.m., a little later than we expected.

As I set up our tent in the campground that was suggested to us, I heard someone in the distance shout, "All hail Ra!" This was the first indication that we had left the world of our ordinary experience and stepped into another.

Throughout the festival I would hear people "all hail" a lot of things and it would lose almost all meaning by the end. But, at that moment when I heard the, "All hail Ra!" it was the beginning of my spiritual journey at the pagan festival.

That moment stood in contrast in my mind to Buddhist mantras.

When children chant, "Om Mani Padme Hum," they often get excited and shout. When adults do it they often sound bland and bored. I wonder why others don't always get as excited about the Dharma as I do. It's an important lesson that we, as Buddhists, can take from the pagan community, I think.

Also, pretty soon I noticed there were a lot of naked people.
About one in every 10 people was exposed. I'm not a puritan by any means—I knew what we were in

for and naked people don't bother me at all. I think our culture has a pretty crazy relationship to nudity and sexuality in general. People freak out about wardrobe malfunctions while at the same time one of the biggest industries in America is porn.

Anyway, I'm getting off track. Nudity doesn't make me uncomfortable. That's my point.

We got there just in time to set up our tent and then eat. There was a band performing and I thought they were pretty good. They were playing a song that was a little comedic, with pagan inside jokes, some of which I got and some I didn't. There would be other bands performing throughout the festival, but I thought this one was the best.

Then we went to go see a bonfire.

There's a fire circle in the campground, not too far from our campsite. We headed there and saw naked people dancing around a giant fire, whilst drums were being played. When one imagines pagan camp, maybe this is what they think of.

I would see this exact thing the next three nights in a row, but that first night it was really special. My wife and son went to bed in our tent and I stayed by the fire, watching the dancers. I just listened and stared in wonder as I watched fire dancers move through the night. It was special.

Friday morning I took the long walk to the showers. The showers were about a fifteen minute walk from our campsite. And down a long wooden staircase. I counted the stairs—there were 72. This was also the location of the only real bathrooms.

This was the first time I went to a co-ed shower. A big open shower room, like the ones in gym class. For men and women. I was up early, so it was just me and another man taking a shower together that day, although a couple arrived as I was leaving.

The whole camping trip I kind of hoped a hot girl would show up and shower with me. Nothing more than showering, of course. I'm married. But showering with a strange beautiful woman would be a neat experience.

There was also a private shower room, but it was small and looked uncomfortable. I wasn't interested. I'm not modest, so I wasn't worried about showering with people. My wife would end up going to that private shower room every time she took a shower and I don't judge her for that.

I left my family at camp to go to a Chakra and Aura Cleansing Workshop.

I'm a little skeptical about such things but I wanted to have more of the pagan festival experience.

It was in a spot called the Bardic Circle, a circle a little smaller than the one where I had seen a fire the night before. This is where I would be giving my teachings in just a few hours.

Surrounding the Bardic Circles, there were vendor tents. Vendors come from far away to sell their hippie and pagan gear at the festival. I saw books and sarongs and incense and some really cool meditation cushions with zippers (the covers could be taken off and washed, like pillow cases, which seemed like a genius invention, but the creator of these didn't have a business card to give me and I didn't have $40 to spend, so I can't tell you where to get these).

Anyway, the workshop wasn't what I expected.

I thought a person would cleanse our Chakras and Auras (whatever that means).

Instead, they taught us how to cleanse them for one

another. The guy in charge said, "Everyone choose a partner, someone you do not know." There were about 10 of us. I turned to an attractive topless woman and said, "Hey, do you—" but before I could finish the sentence she was gone, partnered with another woman.

I like to pretend she didn't hear me. It's less embarrassing that way.

I ended up paired up with a nice older lady. They showed her how to feel my aura and clean it. She said, "Wow, there really isn't a lot to clean here. Your aura is pretty good." I thanked her awkwardly for what I thought must be a compliment.

She asked me if I was into meditation or something. I told her I was but didn't get into the fact that meditation was why I was here at the festival. I found it a little amusing that she asked me that, though.

Then it was my turn. I was a little nervous about this because I didn't think I'd be able to feel an aura. I closed my eyes and tried to feel for her aura and she spoke up.

She said, "Don't bother. You won't be able to feel mine. I'm on painkillers for my back. My aura can't be felt." I had dodged a bullet. I wouldn't have to worry about whether or not I could feel auras or clean them. I was happy when this workshop was over because the sun was bright and it was getting hot.

I returned to camp and spent quality time with my wife and son.

By the way, my son made a lot of friends at this festival. There were a lot of little boys for him to play with. I think he had a better time than either of us, and we had a great time. There were some boys in our campground that he played with and some other boys up in the vendor area that he played with too while we looked around at the shops.

A few hours passed and it was time for my first workshop. I was nervous.

I wasn't ready. I was still a stranger in a strange place and I was not comfortable.

I think I did fine, but I could have done better.

I wanted to teach without notes, so I went in without any notes. I was worried that if I had something to read, I would just be sitting there reading to my audience and I thought that would be very impersonal.

I was given a little headset and microphone so that I could be heard. We were, as I said, right by the vendor area and there were things going on around us. And in the distance, we could hear drums being played.

There were about 25 people around me.

Four of them were actually people I already knew.

This was my workshop on meditation practice and I talked about meditation for a while.

I'll try to summarize what I said here. As I said, I was working without notes, but I have a pretty good memory of the experience, so I can remember what I said pretty well.

I opened with a joke. It was, "People say when you're nervous, you should picture your audience naked. I'm having a really easy time doing that here."

That got a lot of laughs, especially from the people in the audience.

This was a hot day and people were just trying to be comfortable. This is a place where that's allowed, so who could really blame them.

Anyway, here's what I said. I didn't work from notes, but I wrote down all the key points when I got back to my tent.

"Meditation is not a magical practice. Anyone can do it. I'm selling water by the river, because you could have figured this out on your own very easily.

It's a way of tuning in to ultimate reality. It's been shown to improve focus, mental and emotional stability, lower blood pressure and increase compassion.

I'm a true believer in meditation. Some people aren't and that's okay. There's a quote from the Dalai Lama that has turned into a meme on the internet. It's, "If every eight year old was taught meditation, violence would disappear from the world in one generation." I believe that is true. Meditation can be incredibly transformative.

I recommend daily meditation, but that's a big struggle because of how many distractions are available in the modern world. I could meditate or I could watch Netflix. We seem to think we have a right to be entertained all the time.

So, I'm going to have meditation groups around the city. If you have trouble meditating at home or you just want a group, come meditate with me."

I handed out some business cards saying, "This isn't so you can call me and ask me to come your house and meditate with you, although if you ask I probably will, this is so you can add me on Facebook and start reading my blog."

"So, what are we trying to do?

We're trying to control our discursive thoughts. Our minds are crazy, always jumping around, rarely truly focusing on what we're doing. An example I like to talk about is driving. When we're driving our cars, we often aren't focusing on what we're doing. We are not only messing with our phones or radios, but also we're thinking about where we're going or where we've been. People get in car accidents all the time because they aren't paying attention to the damn road.

If we train ourselves to focus, a wonderful transformation begins.

If we can train ourselves to be more present then we can experience more joy from positive and neutral experiences and we can more truly understand that negative experiences are temporary and that makes them easier to deal with."

Now, at this point, I did open it up for questions and there were none, or at least none that stick out in my memory.

For some reason I assumed that 30 or 40 minutes had passed, so I thought we would meditate for 20 minutes and then my hour long workshop would be over. I didn't bother to look at the time.

Because I was nervous, i.e., not facing the situation with equanimity, I messed up.

So, I set the timer on my phone for 20 minutes, again I could have very easily checked the time and seen that it was 4:15, but for some reason I didn't, and we started meditating. I could have done a 40 minute meditation just as easily.

Twenty minutes went by and I said, "Well that about completes our hour together…"

And someone in the audience spoke up and said, "Um…it's 4:35"

I think I appeared calm, but my mind was in a panic. I wondered what I would do for the next 25 minutes.

I said, "Are there any questions?"

There were none.

So, I taught them the Om Mani Padme Hum mantra and we chanted it. Then we chanted it again, slowly.

Then I led a walking meditation for about 10 minutes.

Then we came back to a sitting meditation. There were only 10 minutes left to fill, so I set my timer for 10 minutes and we meditated.

Knowing it was the end of my workshop, my wife and son approached the vendor area. My son approached and yelled out, "Daddy!" and ran up and climbed on me.

I said, "Well when my son shows up, I know meditation time is over."

In my head I was freaking out. I thought this was absolutely a terrible performance on my part. I thought I would have done better if I had had notes.

One of the guys in my audience, an old friend of mine, said to me, "You need to slow down and relax."

He was right.

That night we spent some quality time with the people in our camp and later watched another bonfire.

I should note right now that every night we went to bed at my son's bedtime. We didn't really party at this camp. It would likely have been a very different experience if my son hadn't gone with us.

As I went to sleep in my tent, I wondered how my second workshop would go.

That night it rained. When I woke up in the morning it was raining lightly and there was mud everywhere. I put on my water shoes. I had brought them for lake swimming. As it would turn out, we didn't go swimming, but water shoes come in handy when walking in mud.

So, I walked down to the showers and took a shower. I was completely alone this time.

My mood darkened. The rain and the mud were getting me down. My second workshop was to come at 2:45 on this day, Saturday, and I wondered if it would get rained out. I was nervous because of

219

the first one. Although, I should note, everyone told me the first one was good. So my own harsh self criticism may have been a factor in this.

The rain cleared up after lunch and my wife and son laid down for a nap. I went for a walk. I still had a couple of hours.

I went for a walk in the woods.

I was feeling down, weather gets me down sometimes.

I stood, alone in the woods, just thinking about my day and pondering. I accidentally brushed against a tree and suddenly the world opened up to me. I believe I had what they call a Kensho experience. In my view, enlightenment consists of many little enlightenment experiences, called Kensho, where the body and mind drops away for a short time and oneness is attained. After many of these Kensho experiences, ultimately true enlightenment is attained.

Others believe that Enlightenment comes all at once and I respect that opinion, but I disagree.

Some people aren't going to like that I'm writing

about this. There are those in the Buddhist community that think that talking about mystical experiences is unhelpful. I've written controversial articles before, it doesn't bother me.

I think it's helpful to talk about our experiences.

Phillip Kapleau's book, The Three Pillars of Zen, has several stories about such experiences and it is a pretty well liked book on the subject of Zen, I think.

There I was, standing in the woods, and suddenly I was gone. There was just the woods and the trees and the mud and the bugs and drumming in the distance, which didn't sound quite so far away in the context of this experience. This is hard to describe. Sometimes words fail. Bodhidharma said that the truth is, "Beyond words and letters."

I've had a handful of such experiences in my life and each time I bring a little bit more back with me when I return.

I had the experience of being one with the mud and the trees, one with everything around me. One with the voices I could hear yelling out things like, "Trash pirates are coming!" One with the birds in the sky. One with the sun that was making me warm. I experienced oneness and emptiness at the same time. I touched my Buddha-nature, the empty mind ground. Time lost all meaning, but only a few minutes passed.

I returned to my self with a completely different view. I was suddenly inspired. I rushed back to my tent, careful not to wake up my wife and child, and grabbed a notebook. I wanted to have notes for my second talk. I knew that if I didn't, I would leave something out. What I really wanted was to give my talk right then and there, but it was still two hours away, so I sat and wrote instead. This was the opposite of what I had done the first time, but that's okay. I felt like the first workshop hadn't gone well.

I was walking on air, dwelling in a state of bliss. I remember giving my talk, but things are a little hazy, like a remembered dream.

Here is a summary of what I said.

I divided my talk in terms of the three jewels.

1) Buddha

The Buddha was originally a prince named Siddhartha Gautama who ran away from home. He was given every possible luxury, but he was an especially sensitive person, so he was really troubled by suffering, old age and death. He decided to leave his life and go on a spiritual journey. At this time period in India, this was a pretty common thing to do.

He started what I call a Spiritual Revolution. He studied with several spiritual teachers. He found the mainstream religion of the day to be anti-science and hostile to women, minorities and the poor (good thing we don't have to deal with that today). So, he went into the wilderness to find teachers of alternative religions. He learned yoga and many meditation practices, as well as self-denial.

He sat under a tree. He decided he would sit until he had fundamental insights. He realized that, ultimately, the truth was within himself, and within all of us.

There's a famous quote from him that says: "The way is not in the sky. The way is in the heart."

What he realized was Buddha Nature. This historical figure isn't the Buddha we really want to talk about. The one we really want to talk about is the one within ourselves.

We just have to tune in to the truth. It's expressed in

two seemingly contradictory ways, but that's only because we are using logic instead of intuitive thinking.

Buddha Nature is the idea that we are already enlightened. We just have delusions that prevent us from realizing our true self. The message is that separation isn't real. We are all one with our environment and each other. The things that separate us, labels and social boundaries, are artificial and they prevent spiritual growth.

Emptiness is the idea that I am nothing. That is, it's often better to think of myself as part of a whole rather than as an individual.

Is there a difference between being nothing and being everything? Other than the fact that one sounds positive and the other sounds negative?

2) Dharma

The Buddha called his teachings a Middle Way. He believed that fulfillment wasn't to be found by indulging in all of life's pleasures. It also wasn't to be found by denying ourselves all of life's pleasures. It was somewhere in the middle.

His teaching consisted of training in three things:

morality, concentration, and wisdom.

Morality: don't be a jerk. We have an ego but let's try to live as though we don't. Everything we do to try to make life better for self and others. This is important because being a greedy jerk all the time strengthens the ego and we are trying to soften the ego. Being kind helps tear down the barriers between self and others.

Concentration: Our lives are better if we just pay attention. A transformation begins if we just notice the world. We are distracted all the time and it doesn't serve us well. Often the only time we are in the moment is if we're having sex or doing some kind of art. Often we are missing out on our lives. Learning how to be here now is important.

Wisdom: Cultivating an intuitive understanding that we are part of a whole, not a fundamentally separate individual. Deep meditation as well and mindfulness of the world around us takes us there. I won't lie to you. When I stub my toe I don' t say, "Oh pain is rippling through my body, I am part of a whole, not an individual, so I am not suffering." I'd like to be that way, but I'm not.

He defined the nature of existence with the three

characteristics:

Suffering, Impermanence and non-self.

Suffering: As the Rolling Stones say: "You can't always get what you want." We want things and there are things we want to get rid of. Life will never be perfect.

Impermanence: Everything changes. Things we like come and go, as do things we don't like. In the grand scheme of things nothing lasts long. We often don't think of things this way.

Non-self: You don't have an independent existence. We can't describe ourselves in any meaningful way. We are a collection of things just like a car or anything else.

4 Noble Truths:

1) suffering

2) caused by not understanding/delusion

3) we can get out of suffering

4) by transforming ourselves.

How?

I recommend silent meditation. It's a way to train

our minds to do what we want. Do you have trouble sleeping at night because you're thinking too much? Meditation helps.

Silent meditation is my practice. It's what I do and what I teach. But there are other Buddhist methods such as: mantras, visualizations, riddles, and mandalas. All of these are good too.

I recommend meditating at home every day. But if you can't or won't do that, you can always come sit with me. I went to a Buddhist temple for a long time before I really could get myself to do it on my own.

3) Sangha

Spiritual community. The Buddha said we should have others on the path with us. I like that because if we're doing it on our own, then if we skip a meditation no one will know. It's like a support group; It's considered a sangha any time practitioners are doing practices together. So, we are a Heartland Pagan Festival Sangha right now. If I am asked to come back next year, we will be again.

—-

When it was over there was a lot of applause. I

opened the group for questions.

A man asked me if there were gods in Buddhism. I said, "The short answer is no. But, the different branches of Buddhism have very different characteristics. Some of them do look up to spiritual beings called Bodhisattvas. These are probably very similar to what pagans would think of as gods or spirits. Some people believe these Bodhisattvas are real and some look at them as metaphors."

I told them about the most well known Bodhisattva. The one who is a male called Avalokitesvara in India, but is a female named Kuan Yin in China.

They knew about her already. Kuan Yin is well known in goddess worshiping communities, I think.

I was surprised when a woman asked me about meditation and autism. I told her that some of the kids I teach at the Rime Center Dharma School have autism. Parents always tell me that it works wonders for their kids.

Someone asked me if it's okay to practice Buddhism alongside other religions. I said that it was. I know some Buddhist pagans and Buddhist Christians. Buddhism allows such things.

I handed out business cards again, as I had the first time. Some people from the audience gave me hugs.

My responsibility at the camp was over. I could simply enjoy it now. I was full of nothing but joy.

Sunday was dry. I went to a workshop called Love Within, while my son went to go pretend to be a pirate.

Love Within was a good workshop. It was run by a woman and her basic message was: if the divine light that is one with everything is within us, then we're never alone. We are always with that divine light. Not exactly the same as Buddha Nature, but it matches what I believe very well.

I was there for another night and we packed up and left Monday morning. It took hours to pack up our things and leave, by the way. By the time we left I was sunburned on my back and shoulders because I spent a good part of Sunday walking around shirtless.

By the end I felt like I was home, like this was where I belonged.

It's worth noting that great spiritual teachers like Buddha and Jesus happened to find the spiritual experiences they were looking for in the wilderness.

It rained again Sunday night, so it was muddy when we were packing, but the mud didn't bother me so much anymore.

I had had a spiritual experience. I had found enlightenment at pagan camp, although the only enlightenment you find there is the enlightenment you brought with you.

I haven't written much about the people because, again, I didn't get their permission. I will say the weirdest person I met was a guy in a satyr costume.

And I'll say this. Every person I met there was full of non-judgment and positivity. I've never been in a place so open and loving. These people were Bodhisattvas, every last one of them.

And I brought a little bit of that experience back with me. Pagan camp is part of who I am now. Part of my teaching.

I know lots of Buddhist organizations that have joined interfaith groups or Unitarian Groups. That's fine. There's nothing wrong with that. But I'd rather throw my lot in with the pagans. I'd rather network with them and join their spiritual groups.

Non-judgment, openness, respect for the earth, kindness, love.

Sounds pretty good to me.

ABOUT THE AUTHOR

I**Daniel 'Heng Xue' Scharpenburg** is an
authorized teacher in the Ch'an Guild of Huineng, in
the lineage of Ch'an Master Xu Yun. He continues
to study under Buddhist teachers in several different
traditions. He runs a Buddhist Sunday School for
children at the Rime Buddhist Center in Kansas
City and leads a sitting group called Far Out Zen.

232